The darker its shading on this map, the higher a country's economic development. The criterion for grouping is the percentage of overall production derived from agriculture (including livestock, fishing, and forestry). The lower the share a country derives from its agriculture, the *more* developed it is in industry and services. Compare the United States with Mexico. *Note:* The measure is the percentage of each gross national product contributed by value added during 1994 from all agriculture, including livestock, forestry, and fisheries. Compiled from *World Bank Atlas,* 1996, and *World Resources,* 1994–5.

 No data   >30%   20-29%   11-19%   6-10%   <6%

Reason Enough to Hope
America and the World of the
Twenty-first Century

Philip Morrison and Kosta Tsipis

The MIT Press
Cambridge, Massachusetts
London, England

©1998 Massachusetts Institute of Technology

This book was set in Sabon by Crane Composition, Inc., and was printed and bound in the United States of America.

Library of Congress Cataloging-in-Publication Data
Morrison, Philip.
    Reason enough to hope : America and the world of the 21st century
    Philip Morrison and Kosta Tsipis.
      p.   cm.
    Includes bibliographical references and index.
    ISBN 0-262-13344-X (hc : alk. paper)
    1. Nuclear nonproliferation.   2. Arms control.   3. Security,
International.   4. Nuclear arms control—United States.   I. Tsipis,
Kosta.   II. Title.
    JZ5675.M67   1998
    327.1'745—dc21   98-23561
                                                                   CIP

Contents

A Personal Preface: Blue Sky, Partly Cloudy

One voice missing: Two of us now sign this work, although three began it. It is dedicated to our decisive but silenced partner, who initiated the idea and brought us together. He broadly sketched for us the book's timing, purpose, tone, and universe, but he did not live to put more than a few pages on paper.

That man was our friend Jerome Wiesner, born in 1915, died in October 1994. A few sentences can begin to evoke his life as celebrated citizen, scientist, and educator. As a new electrical engineering graduate of the University of Michigan, he took his first job in 1940, to establish the first recording studio at the Library of Congress, and then worked for a year or so as field recordist for Allan Lomax, noted collector of American folk song. By 1942 he had come to MIT to join the Radiation Laboratory, the wartime center devoted to advancing radar in America. After a brief stay at Los Alamos just at war's end he joined the MIT faculty, where he would rise to professor and then to director of the flourishing Research Laboratory for Electronics, a center in some part heir to the Radiation Lab. His leadership there was conspicuous. Wiesner had always recognized that communication systems include society and its arts as fully as they exploit the enabling technology. Amid a tide of enviable innovations in technique from the big lab, he made it home to the cybernetics of Norbert Wiener as well as to the revolutionary linguistics of a young Noam Chomsky.

In 1961 he went to the White House along with other Cambridge friends and associates of John Fitzgerald Kennedy; he would serve as Kennedy's science advisor throughout the president's term. Wiesner often recounted the dark day in the Oval Office when a reflective president heard clearly from the worried scientist that fallout from distant tests of thermonuclear bombs was being detected in the rain drenching the White House lawn. More perhaps than to anyone else save for President Kennedy, we owe to Wiesner the Limited Nuclear Test Ban signed as part of the Treaty of Moscow, which went into force in October 1963.

That first step toward nuclear peace has been indisputably marked in the very history of Earth's atmosphere by the steady decline of radioactive fallout worldwide as the years have passed without further large atmospheric tests of nuclear weapons. That was the main outcome of the agreement signed by Kennedy on the hard-won "advice and consent" of the Senate, five weeks before the president's sudden death.

Back from a changed Washington as 1964 dawned, Wiesner made his mark at MIT wider and deeper. That more than 40 percent of the 1997 MIT entering undergraduates are women, that MIT arts and humanities are vigorous all the way from modern painting and sculpture to linguistics and music, depend much on his years of active, sensitive, and devoted leadership, first as provost, later as president of the Institute for the ten years from 1970. He raised the first funds to move the Media Lab toward current renown in a distinctive new building, now named for Wiesner and his wife Laya. He never left off his campaign against nuclear weapons. In 1993 Wiesner was honored in Washington with a medal for high public service. Weakened by a brave struggle against the effects of a stroke, he ended his speech with an open appeal, straight from the heart, to those in the room who could—if they would only act—"help slow down the crisis we are in" by addressing the potentially calamitous world arsenal of tens of thousands of ready nuclear warheads.

He faced up to what is real, holding reason high. But he knew that reason and good sense would not prevail among humankind unless partnered by hope, by empathy, and by courage, all traits that were woven into his fiber.

This book began with a conversation between Kosta Tsipis and Jerry Wiesner on a sunlit afternoon in Jerry's second-floor corner office in the Wiesner building. This discussion, full of conditionals and hypotheses about U.S. security in the post–Cold War world, was interrupted when Jerry said abruptly: "Why don't you write a book about 'blue sky'? About what is possible within the broad objective constraints that delimit our options: the laws of physics, energy, and food availability, population, global wealth, geography, weather. Write about possible global security arrangements that would tend toward peace. Write about what is possible and hopeful, about blue sky."

Tsipis objected that scientists do not speculate on approximations of perfection. "In your high-energy elementary particle physics days, how did you plan experiments?" asked Wiesner. Tsipis answered that he would design the ideal experiment and then scale it back to suit the resources at hand. That way, when performing the actual experiment, he would know both what he was driving at and what the limitations were. Halfway through his explanation he realized he had made Wiesner's point. Once again Jerry had the right idea. With his usual generosity Wiesner agreed to work with us on the book, as he did until the very last day of his working life.

Days later physicist Philip Morrison joined physicist Tsipis and engineer Wiesner on the project. Many years earlier Morrison had left the Manhattan Project for the campus, having spent more than four years in Project service as physicist and group leader, from Chicago to Los Alamos, to Tinian, and finally to Japan. Like Wiesner, he was born in 1915, and they had become friends and partners in opinion ever since Los Alamos. But while Wiesner's was manifestly the way of the serious insider, Morrison's was of the political outsider, both more academic and more dissident.

As Wiesner drew away from Washington and closer to MIT, he and Morrison found more and more to agree on in opposing Cold War preparations without limit. When Wiesner phoned Morrison late in 1992 to ask, "Do you know Kosta Tsipis? Can you work well with him?" the answer was yes.

The three of us prepared a brochure, prelude to a comprehensive study, that argued for a step-by-step reduction of military forces by the new Clinton administration. That path had been opened by President Bush when, in 1991, after the Soviet state ended, he ordered the Strategic Air Command to cease emergency preparations to strike, after it had kept a command post airborne every minute for thirty years. By 1992 the president had completed an agreement with the new Russia on cutting the number of strategic weapons in service, and had also unilaterally moved to eliminate U.S. tactical nuclear weapons at sea, and to lower their numbers ashore. Bush would reduce all U.S. forces by a noticeable fraction, though overall their cost in current dollars did not fall but even rose a little.

Our expectations for the new administration were high, but entirely awry. President Clinton took hardly a step along this line until he pursued discussions on a complete ban on nuclear tests at the end of his first term. Nuclear war seemed no longer a pressing public concern, displaced by fevered but secondary debates over the right of homosexuals to serve in the American military and the place of women in the armed forces. Our self-printed proposal in early 1993 for a much-reduced but sufficient U.S. military in the year 2000, which included cutbacks in nuclear and conventional forces alike, found wide and quick rejection. It was condemned by peace groups because it didn't eliminate nuclear weapons and viewed by majority opinion as an unwarranted and insupportable reduction in American prowess.

Despite the swift ascendance of federal budget deficits as a central political issue, no ears were yet ready to hear direct discussion of military cuts. (The annual federal deficit was less than the Department of Defense budget during the decades of the Cold War.) Unfortunately, the simmering local instabilities of the post–Cold War world did not prompt a rational look at the forces the United States might need but rather a bipartisan silence on the entire question, once the path-breaking initiatives of the Bush adminstration took effect. The hostility emanating from a disorderly Somalia, a fractious Libya, and a beaten Iraq seemed to substitute in the public mind for the great confrontation between NATO and the Warsaw Treaty Organization, although patently they were at least an order of magnitude smaller in scale.

But we three continued to prepare a book to treat not only the issues of war and peace far into the twenty-first century, but also other widely recognized complex issues: the growing human population, the need for economic development to reduce global inequities and mass poverty, and the price of continued growth in its drain on specific resources—energy, food, soil, water—and its effects on the global environment. Jerome Wiesner remained a partner in our work well into 1994; less vigorous month by month, that autumn he left us forever.

The entire present text is the responsibility of the two surviving authors.

A Self-Assessment

All three authors were deeply formed by the experiences of World War II, during which Morrison and Wiesner actively participated in developing weapons. Both were 30 years old at war's end; Tsipis was a schoolboy of ten. During five years in wartime Athens, he had witnessed close at hand death by bullet and hunger and the arbitrary violence of armed occupiers. All three, too, were trained in the physical sciences. Naturally we share their general method: a quantitative but approximate analysis that emphasizes the rough quantities involved, searching out persistent and large-scale trends and less concerned with complex and shifting political mechanisms that appear to us more contingent than causal.

We concentrate, therefore, on estimating global probabilities. Individual changes have complex causes, hard to disentangle, remarkably dissimilar from place to place and time to time. The probable is certainly not always that which occurs. Nothing is clearer in history than the significance of leading personalities, of unusual but symbolic events, of shifting alliances, of the chancy vicissitudes of political, economic, and military fortune, of trendy patterns seized upon, often innocently, by the self-serving. We do not even pretend to predict those noisy events in any detail, particularly at global scale.

What we try to do is draw inferences from the most existential of circumstances, often evident physical facts, looking to see where reason and empathy can join in judgment. The "blue sky" approach is optimistic, but it is not blind to the clouds always present. We tease out the possibilities for improvement. We value inclusion over exclusion, and we place peace above unending conflict, though we recognize both that major social interests often sharply oppose one another and that the given institutions can be decisive in an unending variety of ways.

For us the broadest trends seem to converge. The time scale of decades is more coherent than annual changes. It is these we may hope to anticipate. We often see the improbable and even the unreasonable, and still would we argue that in the longer run and for a significant fraction of cases, outcomes will more and more favor the biasing path of reason. The high costs of modern conflict in dollars and in blood favor compromise over the longer run, for few can look to an unalloyed victory.

These pages contain no sermon. We do not expect that all that happens is just what we favor, nor even what we can predict. Events fluctuate, but we write of a system of action, mostly incremental, not with the fruitless hope of "ending history" but to bias the sum of short-term tendencies toward a peaceful and more equitable world a century away. A bias toward reason in the actual circumstances favors such improvements. Just as hopeful ventures may go astray, so bleak cases may in time come to felicitous outcomes. We concede that we are optimists, who see that the limits to reasonable foresight do *not* preclude a hopeful outcome.

We outline only one approximation of a path consistent with the grand physical controls over human life on earth. No socioeconomic systems of thought fully determine that future. Consumption will not grow forever. To most temporal power we expect some counterpower will duly appear. The exclusion of wide sectors of society from a share of power is less likely to succeed as larger populations gain education and cease rapid growth. No ideal society, neither the purity of laissez-faire nor the coming of a fully planned world, appears a likely bet.

Our hopes are founded on recognition that runaway war, runaway human numbers, and heedless use of the global environment must all be avoided for survival. We do not justify our recommendations by moral convictions alone. Our advocacy is heartfelt, but put forward as a rational, approximate answer to existential challenges. Of course what we propose cannot and will not be closely followed. We seek to establish only the plausibility of a workable outcome for our species over the next century.

In all probability our species faces a unique period, marked by the near coincidence of two major end points in human history. We have reached the end of ten or a hundred thousand years of population growth, recently past its overall maximum rate and on the way to a genuine slowdown. At the same time the technology of warfare, itself in rank growth for a few thousand years, has reached mastery of a new realm, nuclear energy for war, opening a regime of potential damage beyond which it cannot physically go, before which it now hesitates. Both of these stunning innovations mark our time, indeed our present decade. No wonder it is a troubled one!

The Cold War thaw opened the chance to look into the long term and across the larger scale. Our project is grounded on that effort. The main measures of our new condition—the count of heads, the specific needs for food, energy, health, and peace, and the environmental impact of our growing activities—are not fully known. But these are dominating and objective circumstances. We begin to hope for a slow engagement more with compelling realities, and less with the dazzling complexities of political action and its emphasis on the immediate that signal this decade of massive transition.

Success is not in any way assured, but from the outset the task we took up was less ambitious and more plausible than full prophecy. We are content if we offer a discerning reader reason enough to hope.

Philip Morrison
Kosta Tsipis
Cambridge, summer 1998

Acknowledgments

First of all, Phylis Morrison. The book would not exist without her work at every level of its creation: logic, emphasis, clarity, visual and textual presentation and execution, and devotion to its contents, its message, its deadline, and one of its creators!

Our indebtedness extends to Larry Cohen, Melissa Vaughn, and Chryseis O. Fox at the MIT Press for their understanding and sensitive professional touch that turned a manuscript into printed pages. Sandra Hackman labored unstintingly to ensure logical coherence and continuity to the sections of the book written by two authors with different styles. Elliza McGrand's stoic yet cheerful support as the manuscript went through several versions smoothed the way to the final product. Deborah Koppald and Asimina Georges, undergraduates from Harvard and Wellesley College respectively, helped with the necessary research.

Finally, we would like to acknowledge the steady support of the MacArthur Foundation that made the writing of this book possible.

1

The Uniqueness of Our Time

It seems a kind of self-centered folly to imagine that one lives in unique times, that history has taken an unprecedented turn. But a greater folly still is to neglect the evidence that history places before us. We therefore open our prospective study of the next century by identifying two major developments in the latter half of this one: the invention and recent retreat of nuclear weapons, and the start of a steady decline in the *rate* of increase of the global population.

The nuclear weapon was an outgrowth of World War II, a genuine and fearful astonishment. After a steady and daunting buildup of destructive power, the American nuclear forces achieved by 1960 full readiness for a major and immediate retaliatory strike even after sustaining a first strike from a nuclear-armed enemy. That readiness was maintained *unbroken around the clock for thirty years*. The ceaseless airborne command rotation on which it rested was brought to an end in 1991, a most eloquent symbol of international recovery from the logic of fear. The real possibility of large-scale nuclear war remained above the distant horizon for more than a full generation. Now this possibility has set, like some balefully glaring planet of evil omen; we can reasonably hope that it will not reappear.

For now, it is nuclear weapons either still unmade or held perhaps in very small numbers by certain irreconcilables that seem a more urgent danger. Some consequences of this transformation in the status of nuclear weapons have been realized: explicit partial reduction by the superpowers in their ready missiles and other strategic carriers, an end to routine targeting of cities, an increased openness both amid the disorder of the former Soviet forces and by design on the U.S. side, the achievement of a total ban on nuclear explosions worldwide, and measures designed to prevent future use of chemical and biological weapons. (The nuclear explosives removed from weapons have so far all been stored in accessible form.) Yet the *unprecedented destructive potential that the tens of thousands of warheads imply remains, unique, unmatched by any newer weapons of mass destruction yet foreseen.* It cannot be ignored in any serious examination of the long-term future of global security.

Can the clear and present easing of this global danger be widened and made lasting? Even though the mutually threatening stance of the great nuclear superpowers has moderated, the shadow of destruction remains as other threatened states have entered the risky game, and as the propensity for arming conventionally has continued. We shall devote a good deal of our discussion to the end game of this long and hazardous competition, and to the establishment of a working system of Common Security among nations.

We shall treat the U.S. military in unusual detail, for we hope to show that the impetus to Common Security, the economic resources to support it, and the first substantial steps toward Common Development all can flow from a major reduction of American military expenditures. U.S. national security would itself be strengthened by the worldwide changes that would ensue.

One other event unprecedented in modern times has taken place: after centuries of increase, *the percentage rate of annual growth in the human population passed its peak between 1967 and 1970, and that rate has declined steadily ever since.* This is a statistical statement from the demographic arm of the United Nations—not a forecast, but a point on a retrospective graph. By now the maximum rate of growth has also peaked on each continent. Africa, the last to pass the peak, saw its rate of population growth decline just before 1990, although it is still the fastest-growing continent.

Commentators focus our attention too seldom on this confirmed decline; indeed, many give quite the opposite impression. Yet that visible maximum in percentage growth rate and its steady decline afterward argue firmly against the explosion of population that many once anticipated. Of course, the overall head count is still on the rise. Since the living population is so large and so youthful, even lowered percentages entail a growing number of new heads; the great ship responds only slowly to the turn of the rudder.

In any time of protracted population increase, the annual *relative* growth rate must peak out earlier, as an arithmetical necessity, than the annual *absolute* increase. But unless the current overall trends reverse, the "population explosion" is behind us. This demographic transition—toward a new world pattern of births and deaths—has been visible for many decades in the industrial countries and is expected to spread worldwide during the decades ahead. Its features are clear: enhanced survival during childhood and adulthood, and in consequence a population whose members are mostly mature or even aging.

We can cite a confirming demographic result that is a little less certain, for it depends on a short-term forecast. *The absolute increment in the number of humans during this very decade of the 1990s is expected to be the largest in recorded history.* (We give the sources for this information and more context in chapter 2 and its footnotes.) The absolute increase is very likely to be smaller in the next decade (or possibly the decadal peak will be delayed only that once). One or the other—either the year 2000 or the year 2010—will mark the end of the largest ten-year increment of heads in all human experience, to be followed by a protracted diminution, a century of approach toward zero growth, or even to a net decline. Runaway population growth will not occur.

Nevertheless, we see three perils ahead. The first is large-scale war. We would not expect a future of much promise were the catastrophe of nuclear war to intervene. We shall outline measures to reduce that now-small probability to the vanishing point in the next two or three decades. Perhaps it will never be easier than today, while intense public fear is still in memory. So we place this goal as the first task—the quickest and the easiest (which is not to say it will be either quick or easy!).

War has been the way of states over their entire history. We believe that an effective end to nuclear war entails a serious effort to limit, fend off, and evade conventional wars, even civil wars, that kill with less extravagant and modern weapons. Otherwise the catastrophe will return, a terrible instability lurking within preparations for larger conventional wars. Nuclear "secrets" are manifestly out, and high technologies proliferate. Prohibition measures are therefore not enough; positive incentives and a sense of evenhandedness must be present in international affairs if proliferation is to be stopped.

We therefore detail an international effort to blunt war though a system of Common Security. We do not expect that our plan, or indeed any other, can extirpate war completely in a few decades. But there is a good chance that the number and especially the scale of wars to come can be drastically reduced by the third decade of the next century.

Our policy will require less effort, less expense, and less time than the large-scale response needed to face the other two perils ahead. Our plan rests on two facts: the commonality of certain security interests among many nations, especially those with much to lose; and military economies of scale. Our approach will reduce individual national military establishments and consolidate them into a sturdy, dedicated force operating under international auspices, probably the U.N. Security Council. These forces, costing a total of perhaps $40 billion a year, would be capable of countering military aggression on a scale that Iraq, oil-rich and long in the planning, deployed against Kuwait and Saudi Arabia in 1991. Some savings would be used to fund nonmilitary efforts to anticipate and allay conflict, some to apply civil sanctions against states that threaten conflict.

We use the U.S. armed services to illustrate how much we can save and how safe we can become under Common Security. Those forces are now the most powerful on earth, especially for the projection of power. We feel at home in this domain, and we are eager to show the impact of recent changes in the technology of war and in widely held attitudes toward war fighting. We show that we can reduce our forces in a decade by one-half to two-thirds, saving a total of $450 billion, while retaining with our tested allies indisputable military superiority over any probable hostile grouping.

In the longer run we discuss how the Common Security system can grow to deter or even to counter most transborder aggression, even nuclear attack against a nonnuclear nation. The cost of this system is so low that it would allow all nations to reduce military budgets below some 2 percent of gross domestic product, saving some $300 billion annually worldwide over the expenses of the early 1990s, when the Cold War ended. But this policy is not mainly budgetary or even humanitarian, or meant to stimulate profitable trade goals, but rather a modern way to achieve effective national and international security. Seeking that security only in isolation, and only by traditional means, is no longer reasonable, if it ever was.

The second peril arises from the unmet daily needs of billions of people.

This danger will steadily rise to demand all attention once populations have peaked in the underdeveloped world after five decades or so. The nearly doubled number of people will need double the food, double the water, and more than double the energy, unless human misery is to grow by much more than double.

We see the needed response as Common Development, which we outline in chapters 8 and 9. Savings from world military expenses under Common Security could enable a modest but strategic down payment on meeting primary needs during the next two decades by raising transfers to the poorer lands threefold or more, to some $150 billion a year. Of course a comparable amount could be used to help end the internal asymmetries that weigh so heavy in the "rich" lands.

This policy is a long-range one and has linkages to security because inequity in growth can become a cause of armed conflict on a scale that is unmanageable. Coercive stability appears more and more as an illusion. Superpowers are fading as the world grows apace. Large national armies commanded by reluctant elites depend on the support of populations likely to become more and more unenthusiastic for distant military exertions. The signs are at hand in most well-armed nations. Certainly the results will be neither universal nor immediate, but we outline a path to its growth.

The third sobering peril is degradation of the global environment. Should it extend to an ecological collapse, large parts of the globe, including areas of the United States, could become only marginally habitable. Pollution of air and water, growing demands upon these resources and upon land and soil as well, not to mention unexpected chemical modification of the ozone-producing layers of the high atmosphere, are all indicated. The demographic transition puts some cap on the damage, but at present we are unable to assess the risks ahead with any confidence. Most uncertain is the risk of far-reaching climate and sea-level modification by the continued accumulation of greenhouse gases, especially of carbon dioxide, the major by-product of fossil fuel consumption. But if we cannot eliminate the potential for nuclear war and exert some control over the frequency and scale of lesser wars—recall the burning oil wells of Kuwait—we shall lack both the resources and the opportunity to confront these profound environmental menaces. We discuss this arena further in chapter 10.

Priorities

It is easy to conjure up an amplifying feedback loop: large-scale war can deny resources to the task of managing the needs of the doubling population. That larger population is itself a source of conflict, even war, surely of speedier degradation. In turn those events exacerbate competition for resources, put off the advent of workable alternatives, and multiply, first, the causes and instances of war, and then its scale. The worst of futures brings a descent into the abyss of instability, until the combat of all against all, even a nuclear Armageddon.

We do not believe such events lie ahead. But we draw on that scenario to set an agenda for addressing our concerns. First, we need to build Common Security in one generation at a much smaller fraction of the global economy than present military expenses represent. Then we need to provide for the unmet needs of a broad population. Because the tasks required to accomplish that goal are more complex and operate at the scale of the entire human economy, real progress beyond a possible emergency damage control will take fully two generations.

Our discussion of these priorities plainly reflects the experience of the authors, physicists old enough to recall the daily terrors of World War II, and citizens all too familiar with 50 perilous years of nuclear policy since. The next generation, which came to awareness after the war years, tends to weigh more heavily the next element on our list—runaway population growth, with many also concerned about inequitable development, the billions of the poor. The youngest generation has grasped the deepest threat to human welfare—the welfare of the planet itself and its intricate web of life.

Overall, ours is a broad-stroke picture, more like a commission report than a specific model for a country or region or a prescription for ideal action. We seek to aim deep enough in time so that while ideas still hidden in the future are hardly foreseeable, the problems set almost existentially by world economic resources, by human needs, and by the environment itself can be estimated rather reliably.

Our models are based more on estimates of the probable outcome of present trends than on what we or others wish to see. We have a strong sense of the constraints and opportunities that lie in the present material state of the world and in the human capacity for change. Political judgments, especially those of short-term importance, are not our topics. Such judgments often lead the discussion to focus closer to near-necessary conditions than to sufficient ones. Of course there will be exceptions, and we will likely miss them.

Social and political institutions are often determining for one time and place. But general constraints induced by larger-scale phenomena, say population, food and its inputs, fuel sources, war, and atmospheric change, tend to affect more places and to endure for longer times. Such issues can often be examined quantitatively and can open objective choices that transcend ideology and politics. That we mainly argue from the more material side of economic and political problems reflects our limitations, but we submit that these may also be a source of strength for our argument.

In general we do not much consider single countries or offer detailed plans for national action. Instead we aim our main arguments at a time scale often of decades, and across many nations, not all of whom will follow the tendency we argue for. Of course this makes our proposals less specific and more suited to a range of outcomes. But existential problems unite solutions in the face of disparate histories, time-honored social structures, even strong predilections. Our approach often elides such details in favor of seeking underlying material constancies that the longer run may uncover. This is a deficiency that more sophisticated political and economic authors may avoid, but we submit that our level of detail may often strengthen the generality of the argument. Special and local causes vary, but outcomes often converge. That is the gain of a statistical stance.

In the end the values we invoke, often only by implication, are ecumenical ones that stem from human experience widely shared among countries and across epochs. While our values do not rest upon any particular authoritative codification, we hope and expect that many readers of diverse views will broadly concur.

High Hopes

The twentieth century was largely marked by a contest between two nominally polar economic modes. One was socialist investment guided by planning under state control, with a definite loss of the feedback loop that comes from the consumers who can in detail accept or reject goods and services offered to them. The other was capitalist, where strong feedback in the marketplaces both for investment and consumption leads to private profit under some measure of regulated competition. The first fails under the dissatisfactions that grow when the planners work on an open loop. The second brings a working system with the propensity to satisfy many, but breeds an unevenness of growth from which many are effectively excluded. The feedback loop works well for those who actively remain in the markets, but more and more people drop out, some even tragically, for a wide set of reasons that center on income and education.

It is no surprise to claim that neither mode was nor is as pure as its theoretical description: no state plan can forever coerce or persuade dissatisfied workers and consumers, and most profit seekers aim to temper the decisions of the market by alliances with state action—or inaction. Reality brings together Japan's Ministry of International Trade and Investment and Sony, the U.S. Food and Drug Administration and tobacco producers, no less than it did the Soviets' ruthless uranium mining enterprises with their postwar spoliation of western Saxony in East Germany.[1]

Are there no markets, multinationals, neglect of externalities, and public welfare in socialist command economies? In market economies, do we not see a web of regulatory law, state grants, subsidies, guarantees, monopolies, protective measures, to say nothing of central banking regulation, laws for bankruptcy, and laws against fraud? The world's work is complex, and nations have their own mixed economies, a tangle too subtle, diverse, and shifting to characterize easily. Rhetoric and theory dim as they encounter reality.

In the United States in particular, one economic model has lately become all but beyond critique. The efficiencies of the marketplace in allocating the profitable use of capital and labor, perhaps in determining all the requirements of production, have become proverbial. There is little doubt that markets often result in measurable economic growth, typically seen in conspicuous changes in the goods on shelves and among many (though not all) of the people. Feedback from buyers' choices to attentive sellers has widely fine-tuned the products they sell.

But markets are rarely inclusive; they respond well only to signals from those with power to buy. Yet the most urgent needs occur among those—

sometimes few, more often many—who lack the average power of purchase. Nor does the feedback extend to matters unseen by buyers: the probity of labels and their claims, for example, is not always to be inferred from their text alone.

We look apart from these matters, however important they may become for social developments within nations. We assign the greatest weight to promotion of step-by-step remedies as the most practical course in a world of old differences under the spreading powers of new technology. We pass over past or present conflicts between economic structures and focus instead on the presently functional extreme (and still increasing) speed and volume of commercial transactions and capital flow worldwide. This is a special multinational phenomenon, akin to the similar social and political influence of world television and telecommunications, of great moment, probably not yet fully understood.

We expect that the world will remain a mixture of compromises; no universal, asymptotic ideal will soon gain adherence. We do argue for informed and less uneven world change, and we estimate its benefits and costs. Certainly costs are not dollars alone; they must take into account values beyond commerce, and effects beyond both buyer and seller. How to do that will become more and more the question as a few people come to hold more of the wealth already so unevenly spread.

The United Nations and smaller institutions as well, from the International Telecommunications Union to the International Monetary Fund and World Bank, mostly evolved out of World War II or were carried over from earlier multinational agreements. These institutions will not remain unchanged—surely, for example, the World War II victors cannot remain the only permanent members of the Security Council as real national power and economic importance shift. But we use the present examples of major international actors anyway, since the problems and many of the means of attack will remain even as the casts of players change.

All these prefatory remarks are meant to induce the reader toward an interpretative view of our proposals. Adjust the ends we seek and the conditions we foresee to include your own favored institutions, whether state agencies, large firms, nongovernmental organizations, planners, or prophets.

It is not our intention or our hope to address ideology or social organization of states a century ahead. We believe that these topics, however important, are not as visible as more existential matters. We would not deny that hopes and dreams of social change or its absence can be prime movers of events. But we limit our concerns to what is written on the wall in the largest characters: war and peace, economic exclusion and inclusion, the flow of the necessities of life, both of information and of goods. The number and kind of soldiers and their weapons, the vital statistics of whole populations, the status and minimal rights of minorities large and small— these seem to demand our attention.

At the same time we postulate a broad goal that unites most if not all lands: the well-being of the entire global population. That is what we try to estimate and then to foster, but of course not by every means. We set peace ahead of war, and we recognize that change is often essential, so we seek means to promote peaceable change in the interest of wider well-being.

Utopia is not our topic, but rather a will to a better world and a description of measures that should lead there. Somewhat utilitarian, our bent is more hopeful than imperative. It is the next approximation that we view as the path. It won't always work; but then we know nothing that will for sure.

Underlying our approach is a conviction that the present state of technology allows, for the next half century at least, a steady growth of economic reward to work well done. This change depends less each decade on specialized resources, on this mine or that port or traditional crop. Change has its costs; who is to pay for the change when it is not, as it certainly will not always be, a mutual gain? The answer is plain: it is the prosperous who will pay. Who else can pay much?

Our ground for hope is simple: those who can pay will, in the name of reason and morality, pay something—while certainly not giving up all their prosperity—to reduce a perceived future risk. A century and more ago the burghers of Bismarck's Prussia accepted a tax burden for measures of public welfare on the wise grounds that state aid to the poor would reduce future threats to health and order. In our world the same argument holds: we can act impelled by fear of war, by the clear and present danger to the shared environment, and certainly also by higher motives of justice and equity. Decisions on how best to proceed will be negotiated within a growing record that will yield both failure and success. Judgment flows finally from the simple but deep fountain of empathy: most people over time, after indifference ends, after envy declines, after redress has passed, seek the fairest ends that most of humankind has long sustained. Our hope is to nourish the sprouts of peace and to weed out the seeds of war.

They who effect improvements can expect overall gain, not only laying up treasure in the heaven of their choice but in stability and widespread peace. Moral and civil unity can grow within a species beset by larger needs to come. Not all will concur, not all will take part; what matters is only that there be enough who will. It is the diverse texture of human events that provides a guarantee.

We hold high hopes, hopes that we believe are supported by reason enough; but indeed, what choice have we?

2
Demography in Times of Peace and War

When the second of those seven seals was opened, St. John the Divine saw a Horseman on a red horse, "and power was given to him that sat thereon to take peace from the earth, and that they should kill one another; and there was given unto him a great sword" (Revelation 6:4).

It has never been difficult to recognize that rider on the red horse: he is named War. History and prehistory join to support the antiquity of war. It is older than writing, as old as human societies of herders and farmers that were able to hold stocks of necessities; only foragers and hunters, usually with little or no store of surplus, seem to have lacked any counterpart to that social license to kill one another we call war, that power borne by the swordsman who rode the red horse.

It is no surprise, either, that the sword he was given as weapon has been multiplied and transformed by the long flourishing of technology among humankind, until today the sword we have forged has grown too great to swing wide on this small planet that bears us all. We cannot omit from a book on war and its future a serious effort to place war not only among the Four Horsemen but also among the less episodic, more customary forms of social interaction. The bewildering wealth and disparity of war's cultural impact—all those helmets, flags, epic poems and stirring anthems, heroes and holidays worldwide—and war's instruments, from the walls of Jericho past the wooden horse at Troy to the cool angularity of the stealthy F-117, bear witness to war's breadth, its demonstrably intoxicating mix of seductive myth and limitless license along with high reason. War indulges blinding anger as it does cooler lifelong plans; it provokes repellent cruelty along with profound and sacrificial devotion, the best and the worst of human behavior.

Our book, an argument for deep change, needs some cool, simple, if necessarily approximate, measure of the consequences of war. For our proposals do not run mainly to human intentions, but rather to their consequences. It is the consequences of war that we address, rather than its moral nature. A concrete measure is a necessity for a cool inquiry. Once we can estimate war's results, its gains and losses, we can better seek out the direction in which societies will tend: when and how will they limit or extend their engagement in war? Our approach requires a rational assessment, not a visceral one. Insofar as war is not mere murder but stems from a social goal widely shared, we search for more general grounds. Certainly our measures are at best crude ones; we must concede frequent exceptions to the claims of reason.

Life Expectancy

Since all humans are mortal, the pale horse of Death cannot alone lead us to a rational judgment on war. That humans should kill one another is judged a misdeed by the consensus of cultures, and yet killing, when socially organized, stands as a widely common practice over time. It is hardly enough to anathematize war: neither the sermons of Jesus long ago nor the recent teachings of Gandhi have had much effect in reducing its incidence. Some rough measure of the price of war in untimely death may help outline a reason for its long and general acceptance among nations.

At its best the measure ought to be social, roughly quantitative, hence probably statistical, and widely applicable. Demographers have devised just such a measure for the average length of life in a given social setting: the *life expectancy*,[1] a measure applicable at any time to any specified group. It is based on actuarial tables that give the current death rate experienced at any specific year of age by the members of the subpopulation for which it is computed. The life expectancy is then simply the average number of years before death comes to any member of that subpopulation (though of course many die earlier or survive longer than the group average). It is calculated for any population from the known deaths by age for a given year, though often these death rates are also averaged over a run of years.

The principle is simple, but the actual task is both tedious and dependent on reliable counts of births and deaths, which are by no means always available. But suppose there exists a credible reckoning for some particular year of the deaths that occur within a nation. Each of these deaths is then assignable to the age of each person whose death is reported. From the census of living persons by age and from this list of deaths it is easy to compute just what percentage of persons at each age die in a given year: 1-year-olds, 2-year-olds, and on as far out as is needed. (It is valuable to have the deaths assigned by gender, since men and women usually differ noticeably in survival.)

Imagine a test sample, say 1,000 individuals representative of the population. Systematically consider the expected chances of survival of that set of persons as they age year after year. Of these 1,000, very few will remain to 100 years of age; some will not survive even the first year. Most will persist for quite a number of years.

Note that this calculation is not only a statistical construction—of course it is inapplicable to any chosen individual—but is not even true to life statistically. For we do not know future survival rates. We must use instead data from some actual past year or run of years, conceding that they will not be precisely what real life will bring in future years. Demography is not prophesy, but a working approximation of what is to come based on past occurrences.

Now take each of the 1,000 representatives on the list. For the first year of life, find what percentage of newborns survive. Continue year by year, using the existing data for 2-year-old survival and so on, with the steadily decreasing sample. Follow all 1,000 to the year of their death, and then add all 1,000 sample life spans together, a few only 1 year, many more at 20, some at 80, and so on. (The universal decline of survival into extreme old age ensures that a few long runs will not much distort the average, although the samples of the very old may become so small that the data are unreliable.) Suppose these add to a total life span of 68,000 years for the whole sample of 1,000, using the real survival rates as tabulated, say, for the year 1990. The resulting expectancy of life for those born in 1990 would then be 68,000 years divided by 1,000 persons, or 68 years.

Today life expectancy is tabulated in detail for most countries. The overall expectancy for someone born in the United States in 1988 was 74.9 years (but an American resident reaching 21 that year could expect an average life span slightly longer than that year's newborns because he or she has survived the perils of childhood). Any residents who had reached the age of 80 in 1988 would on average expect 8.1 years more still, to attain a ripe age of 88, as they would have evaded many more risks. (The usual table ends at age 85; by then calculation has become rather too unreliable.)

A Sample of U.S. Life Expectancies

The expectancy of life in the United States for the year 1988 for certain groups was this:

Newborns	74.9 years
White males at age 21	73.7
All other males at age 21	69.2
White females at age 21	79.6
All other females at age 21	76.7

Overall expectancy is the mean over all groups in the population, weighted by the fractions in each of the categories. For whites of 21 years the number of males and females are about equal, so the overall result for 21-year-old white Americans is close to the simple average of the two, or 76.8 years.

The dynamism of such vital statistics is their most important property. A look at past years will show how much life expectancy itself has risen within the United States, but also how its rise is slowing down. The life expectancies for certain groups born in specific years are listed in table 2.1.

Table 2.1
Changing life expectancies (in years) in the United States

	White males	All other males
1900	48.2	32.5
1920	56.3	47.1
1940	62.8	56.9
1960	67.6	61.5
1980	70.8	65.6
1995 (prelim.)	73.4	65.4

Source: *Statistical Abstracts of the United States*, 1993, table 1174, and National Center for Health Statistics, preliminary data, 1996.

Notice how considerable the social cost of assigned race has been to individual survival in America; most of that cost was borne by infants and children, an enduring effect of African chattel slavery, that congenital defect of our republic.

A good century ago, before modern health standards were widespread, less than 60 percent of all the world's newborns would grow to reproductive age (nominally 15 years). Now within the entire developed world, about 98 percent of them do. (All the current figures in this paragraph are for Italy, representing a typical developed nation; the United States, still afflicted by its congenital defect, has ample room still to better the survival of American children.) Among teenagers in the old days, two-thirds reached 50; close to 95 percent now survive to that middle age. Of 50-year-olds, nearly three-quarters now reach 70, while a hundred years back only a quarter of them ever made three-score-and-ten.

Survival in the developing nations is much less uniform, but in one of the most populous of poorer nations, Bangladesh, only 80 percent of the newborns now reach 15; some 85 percent of their teenagers do survive to 50; of the middle-aged about 60 percent achieve 70. Life expectancy overall is very short there, around 52 years. In no country of the 160 or so whose statistics are published does life expectancy at birth fall below Uganda's level of 42 years or rise above Japan's 79 years for the years 1990–1995.

For the world as a whole the life expectancy at birth is now about 65 years; the developed countries stand at above 75, the poorer world close to 63. An expectancy around 60 years was characteristic of the industrial lands too back in 1930. The lag in demographic change between rich and poor countries is thus about 60 years; during that time the industrial world saw an increase in its own life expectancy of about 10 years. In recent decades the poor world has been able to increase its life expectancy at a much higher pace. A 1-year increase in survival rates during 3 or 4 calendar years of time is what the United States shows at present. But for most developing lands 1 year of gain in life expectancy takes only about 2 calendar years. Of course any gain in expectancy, other things being equal, increases the population; under tolerable conditions longer life is most welcome. Eventually, however, life expectancy will converge to a value (more or less universal) dictated not by calamity or war but by human physiology, or even by choice.

Births and Deaths

Let us tally population change itself in a commonsense way, simply by counting the two terminal events of every life, birth and death. It is evident that the rate of the internal increase in population in a given year is the difference between the rate of births and that of deaths. (For the time being we set aside migration; it usually has only a small effect, a fraction of 1 percent a year. Migration into the United States is not yet an exception to that rule of thumb, though it is becoming increasingly significant.)

The current values of these vital rates are revealing. In the United States there are now each year about 1.4 births per hundred of population, and about 0.9 deaths per hundred population. The growth rate of U.S. population is 0.8 percent per year. Just 0.5 percent are from the cited "natural" excess of births over deaths, and about 0.3 percent more from net immigration. In 1930 the data for the United States were quite different: births, 2.1 percent per year; deaths, 1.1 percent per year; immigration, 0.2 percent per year. The U.S. growth rate in 1930 was then 1.2 percent annually.

In 1995 there were 4.5 billion people in the poorer world, and about 1.2 billion in the richer. Each year about 140 million are born worldwide, and 50 million people die. The population is slowly aging, both overall and in each of the continents; worldwide about 32 percent of us now are children below reproductive age, about 62 percent men and women of working age from 15 to 65, and 6 percent are over 65.

The developed world shows in 1990 a growth rate of 0.5 percent per year, about that of the United States apart from immigration. Births are at about 1.5 percent per year and deaths at 1.0 percent per year. In contrast, in the developing world birth rates are about double the U.S. value, at 3.0 percent, but death rates are about the same, 1.0 percent. Thus net growth is large, at just under 2.0 percent. But that rate of net relative growth[2] has fallen steadily if slowly since it peaked around 1970, at about 2.5 percent per year.

That has been the history of the percentage rate of growth. Of course while the population is growing, even a fall in the percentage rate does not necessarily mean a decrease in the total number of people added to the count every year, since an ever larger global population increases by the percentage rate. But now even the numerical increase in human heads, not

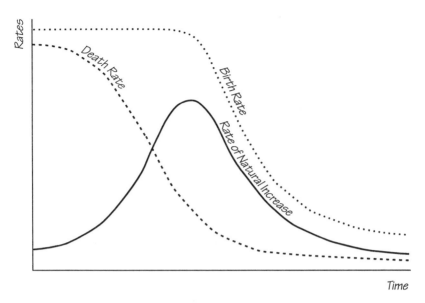

Figure 2.1
The global events leading to a stable world population are diagrammed. The population of the Earth increased as the death rates fell, while birth rates continued high. Once birth rates diminished drastically, the rate of natural increase of the population was also reduced, leading to a stable world population.

the percentage rate, gathered decade by decade, has probably peaked in the 1990s. The all-time high in population increase will likely come in this decade, and the increase is forecast to fall steadily thereafter.

Figure 2.1 tells the story: the swift increase in global population in the twentieth century is a unique, transient phenomenon. Technology, medicine, improved social organization, and better living conditions reduced the overall rate of deaths, mainly of infants and children worldwide, while the rate of births continued high over the span of only two or three generations.

The People: Demography's Best News

By now every continent *has passed its maximum rate of population growth*, as has the world overall, as figure 2.2 shows. The rate of African population growth plateaued latest of all, just before 1990. This great fact, a confirmed and steady decline in the growth rate of world population overall, is without doubt the most important news and about the best news that demography can give. It is the confirmed passage over the historical peak rate of growth and the steady decline since that argues against runaway population growth ahead.

True, absolute human numbers are still on the increase. Since the living population is so high and so youthful, even the lowered rates still result in a large number of new heads. But the rates fix the determinable future as long as the well-marked trends do not reverse. The population "explosion" is past, and the growth of these past years is simply coasting. It takes a long time to turn a great ship, but the rudder has already had its first effects.

The established narrowing of the gap between births and deaths is proceeding much more rapidly among the poor nations than it did earlier in Europe, Japan, and America. As cited above, the decline in net growth is in many lands twice as fast as it was during the nineteenth century in Europe. It has not yet been completed, but we can expect that the persistent signs will be fulfilled. This is in spite of the fact that economic development is by no means so rapid, save over the last few years in China.

The explanation for change in vital statistics has always been that it correlated with economic development. In fact, the signs are now that even countries that are not economically developing can nevertheless enter into the new birth-death regime. The causes are of course less than certain, but contributing factors are surely the fast pace of urbanization, the improved status of women in some lands, the widened availability and enhanced safety of contraceptive techniques, and the speedy flow of ideas and information in this era of radio, TV, and even air travel. Even one returned villager can report on the new world out there. Development, birth control, and education all matter, particularly among women.

Deep worldwide demographic change is in rapid progress. The populous poorer lands, and many smaller ones as well, are generally following the well-recorded history of Europe and America into what is called the demographic transition: a regime marked by many fewer births, fewer deaths, and increased life expectancies. Age distributions are thus necessarily also seeing swift change. During the time of transition, age distributions differ sharply from nation to nation, even among regions. Africa, for instance, now has the youngest people: about 45 percent are now children, and only

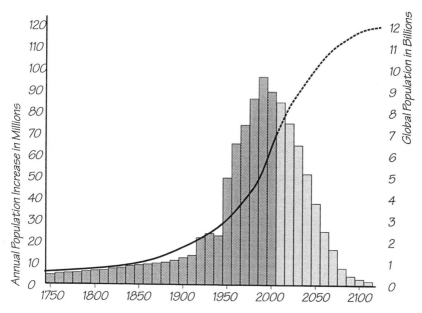

Figure 2.2
Two related graphs appear in one field. The annual global population increase
in millions is represented by the bar graph. The total global population (right-
hand scale) is shown by the solid line. As the annual increase in number diminishes
(it reached its maximum in the 1990s), the total population levels off.
Source: T.W. Merrick et al., *World Population in Transition*, Population Bulletin,
1990 (New York: United Nations Population Division), and UNDP update. See
also WHO Annual Report 1996/1998 for updates.

3 percent are persons over 65. Europeans now include only 20 percent
children, but people over 65 number 14 percent there. (The social implications for the next 50 years are manifold in both circumstances; consider
for a moment schools, the work force, soldiers, pensioners . . .)

These simple numbers justify a note of optimism. What people called the
"population explosion" has turned out to be the worldwide demographic
transition instead. A population plateau lies ahead. Our problems abound,
but we can maintain reasonable hope for besting them, in a world made
more predictable by its stabilizing population.

A remarkable series of publications by S. P. Kapitza, a well-known Moscow physicist, long interested in the stability of the behavior of plasmas,
has revealed an astonishing simplicity in the world growth of population.[3]

A simple nonlinear equation turns out to fit the world head count very well over the two or three centuries for which we have reasonable quantitative information, and forecasts a plausibly slowed growth ahead. The same fit works at least roughly as far back as we conjecture, say a million years.

No one has yet offered a clear explanation for this simplicity. It may be merely an accident. If it is more than that, it suggests that the rise of human population will slow to a limit that is not very far beyond the present number. This limit does not depend explicitly upon crops or contraceptives or family values or any other cultural influence. It is somehow internal to the species, stemming from the many feedbacks—all the many causes— that have led us all without conscious understanding to the overall behavior. (Demographers do not sympathize at all with any such theory, but many physicists, like us, are warily impressed!) This is not unlike like the nature of human language, now widely held to be partly an intrinsic function of the brain, although in this case too the subtle unity underlies an amazing variety of detail.

If this find is of lasting validity, it would much strengthen the empirical conclusion: the once apparently runaway growth of midcentury is moderating into a slow rise toward some ultimate internal limit.

Calamity Old and New

The social calamity paid out to the cruel demands of the Horsemen in the form of war, famine, and pestilence declines nowadays just as does the everyday toll of death in the "normal" course of life. Figure 2.3 shows the crude death rate for the country of Sweden between 1740 and 1920. (Few data from so long ago are as complete as those we have from Sweden.) Before 1820 the figure shows three deadly peaks, each a few years wide, during which death rates more than doubled owing to war, poor crops, and civil war. As the century passed, all those grim peaks fell because of two steady trends—a slowly falling baseline and the still-faster-falling higher curve that joins the occasional peaks.

Order had taken over from calamity. Indeed, the data show a remarkable tenfold decline in the *variation* of the death rate over the years. The annual death rate had approached 5.0 percent in the 1770s, although even in the eighteenth century it would fall as low as 2.0 or 2.2 percent during the

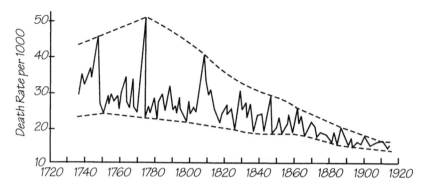

Figure 2.3
Decline in the variation of death rates in Sweden. Famines, epidemics, and wars caused the peaks in the death rate in 1740, 1770, and 1810. As these causes were eliminated, not only did the overall death rate fall, but the variations from year to year were dampened. Survival became almost predictable.

most favorable years. During the last half of this twentieth century the annual death rate in Sweden has fluctuated from a high of 1.3 percent to a low of 0.95 percent. Where once some years brought death at rates increased by 250 percent, now no bad year increases human losses by more than 35 percent. The long French record is similar; death rates there in the 1730s and 1740s varied between 3 percent and 5 percent. Two centuries later the French death rates too were down by a factor of three or four. But the variation between the best years and the worst was reduced by a factor of fully seven.

Today in most years in most nations the rates of death do not change much from year to year. The new regime has begun, a time substantially relieved from the fear of widespread sudden death by famine, pestilence, or war. The Horsemen still call on far too many homes; they take hungry infants lacking inoculations, poor young mothers, overworked and tired farmers, and young soldiers too. But most deaths, however avoidable they might become by a better social ordering of human life worldwide, now appear statistically routine, foreseeable along the expected trend, a trend that with good luck and some semblance of good government will decline over the years. The plots of all the vital numbers are smoother now, and few show the fateful spikes of the past. Certainly calamity has not vanished. Pestilence, famine, and war are starkly visible on the picture tube, monthly if not daily, but with the dreadful exception of wide nuclear war, they do not much influence the trends of the grand demographic transition—a problematic but ultimately cheerful conclusion.

A look at some striking cases of calamity in the past will illuminate our times by comparison. The closing years of World War I were marked by a world pandemic of an exceptionally virulent strain of flu virus called Spanish influenza, almost surely not from Spain but from East Asia. Whereas robust adults survive the usual flu, which is mortal mainly for children under 10 and for patients over 50, the same viral disease from 1917 to 1919 caused a mortality that peaked among young adults between the ages of 19 and 30.

Americans suffered greatly.[4] In the fall of 1918 the scores of big camps where more than 10 million young men were newly assembled to train for war in France were struck hard by the disease. A third of the men in any camp fell ill at the same time, hundreds of them dying daily. It was no different in civil society. From Alaska to Florida, on shipboard even, everywhere, the disease struck mainly the active. The death rate grew monstrously within months. Yet by the end of 1919 the scourge was mostly over. Some 600,000 Americans lay dead from flu, ten times the U.S. losses on the battlefields of World War I, four times the rate of World War II losses, and more than twenty times the sad yearly rate from AIDS. Even the gross death rate reflected this loss plainly, rising to 1.8 percent in 1918 from 1.4 percent the previous year, and falling again in 1919. Life expectancy fell from 51 years in 1917 to 39 years in 1918, and rose back up to 55 during the next year or two. Battle deaths took a little more than a year out of the dozen years of life expectancy lost in 1918. The rest was attributable to the flu.

The plague of current times, AIDS, is slower to kill than war, but it is enduring. It will probably reduce life expectancy overall by under three months, but that reduction will persist for decades. By the mid-1990s about 16 million people had been infected worldwide by HIV (and many of them have died) since it appeared around 1980; a similar death toll is still to come in a decade or so. Yet 20 million worldwide died from influenza in only two or three years.[5] A somewhat similar estimate in the 10 million range can be given for smoking-related lung cancer, a slow, more widespread chronic affliction. (Annual smoking-related losses of life in the United States presently exceed the *total* from alcohol and drug abuse, auto accidents, murders, AIDS, and fires.[6])

Famine remains a powerful killer, usually as the cruel outcome of a chance cabal between social disorder and local flood or drought. Somalia was a timely example, but the most terrifying famine for hundreds of years was suffered in the middle of this century within the People's Republic of China. Ruinous crop weather arrived just at the time of the profound and eccentric reorganization of rural life, dubbed the Great Leap Forward, that occurred from 1958 to 1961.[7] The government suddenly enforced the collection of village households into communes of more than 5,000 people each, without adequate preparation. The villagers were required to farm and even to cook and to dine together, and given the extra task of making steel in their farmyards. When poor harvest and flooding disrupted normal crop cycles, the system had lost its traditional resilience, already hardly sufficient for the challenge. It seems possible that the tragic conditions in some provinces were not even reported to the central authorities, so no relief was dispatched to them. It is certain that the true statistical picture was withheld from publication for two decades.

The numbers that describe this tragedy, now available, are frightening. The death rate in China in 1958, at 1.8 percent per year and falling rapidly, suddenly burst all bounds. It rose precipitously to about 4.5 percent per year in 1959, and fell again by the end of 1962 to about 1.4 percent per year.[8] This mortal peak resembled the grim experience of Sweden during its worst years in the eighteenth century, this time occurring in a nation of more than 600 million people. Some 25–30 million people died in the disaster. The birth rate fell disastrously as well during the same years, so that in the end about 25 million births were lost or at least postponed. The calculated expectancy of life fell from about 46 years in 1958 to a low of 25 years in 1960! It has risen steadily ever since; already by 1962 it was back to 54 years, a little higher than before Mao's Great Leap. In 1990 it stood at 70 years and rising. Indeed, the vital statistics of today's rapidly and unevenly developing China rank it among the developed nations in spite of its still low overall income.

The Twentieth-Century Toll of War

Wars, too, are episodic and calamitous threats to life expectancy. Every life lost in war is a calamity to one person struck and to all those in direct relationship to the victim. But the social calculation emphasizes the long-

run and areawide impact rather than that sudden blow. We use this somewhat distanced account not because we intend to minimize empathy, but
because we are trying to examine the nature and effects of war broadly
over space and time.

Like increasing populations, large-scale war is a salient demographic
feature of our century. Scholars have given us a reasonable census of the
toll of all wars, and use of their data yields the summed and rounded results
in table 2.2.

A century of terrible war has brought more than 100 million excess
deaths. Spreading the effects of war as widely as possible, we see that loss
of life to war in this century averaged under 1.2 million lives per year, a
little more than 2 percent of the total averaged death rate of 55 million per
year. Loss of life span among civilians is distributed in age more or less as
the whole population; losses from military activities affect mostly men
around 20. With such figures, we reckon the overall reduction in life span
caused by twentieth-century war overall. A rough estimate comes from
simply taking the fact that war deaths end in a given year the lives of about
2 percent of the population. That amounts to less than 1.5 years out of the
present world life expectancy of almost 65 years.

Set next to that effect of war another estimate: even today in the United
States poverty entails a 10-year loss in life span, while being black means
a few years' loss in addition. Yet U.S. life expectancy overall has grown
during this century by more than 20 years. In so detached a view War's
horseman, taking a toll of less than 2 years, seems unimportant. It was
fully made up within a decade.

For us this unexpected result goes some considerable way in explaining
a central paradox of the long quest of reformers to bring an end to war.
Why has peace not made more headway over all these centuries? A statistical

Table 2.2
War-related deaths (civilian and military)

War	Deaths	Populations most at risk
World War I	23 million	Europe and Russia
World War II	56 million	Europe, Russia, East Asia
All smaller wars, 1900–1990	30 million	Worldwide

reply is cold but simple: the demonstrated risk of war to life is unimportant when viewed over a wide stretch of space and time. A rational calculation would find that other vital needs—water, food, clothes and fuel, shelter, medical care—come first for most people in a poor world. Even today 2 billion people, from the Bihar to the South Bronx, are either marginal subsistence farmers on tiny farms or almost equally marginalized dwellers in the mean streets and tenements of a hundred fast-expanding cities. As long as national leaders see some compensatory gain from making war, such as acquiring wealth by taking it by force from another, it is a cruel but not an unreasonable policy in a grimly cold calculus of life and death. Of course fear of loss in war plays a role perhaps more important than hope of gain. Redistribution of wealth, opportunity, security, and influence are not well achieved by war. People need an alternative approach compatible with the hopes for stability.

World Nuclear War

All of us have just passed through a long threat of war at an entirely new scale, its intensity disclosed even in embryo by just those two bombs at Hiroshima and Nagasaki. From the 1960s on, superpower preparations for a new level of warfare implied the clear potential for a catastrophic nuclear World War III, with a loss of life to fallout and fireball from three to five times all the losses of World War II, ending 200–300 million lives inside months. If those losses had spread out over North America and the former USSR (and we set aside the likely heavy toll in much of China and Japan downwind), they would have produced an unprecedented sudden drop in life span in these two prosperous lands to below 50 years. That would have meant a sharp historical setback to late-Victorian life spans, without secure hope of quick recovery while fallout and related consequences remained a threat, and with possible deleterious effects upon climate spread even more widely. The destruction of human and industrial resources in the developed nations would without doubt cause scarcities around the world and additional loss of life we cannot predict, even approximately.

As we detail in chapter 3, such effects could follow a nuclear exchange that uses fewer than 5 percent of existing nuclear weapons. The probability of such large-scale nuclear war has certainly lessened since 1991, but the likelihood of widespread destruction if an exchange were to occur remains unacceptably large.

The optimistic message of this book stands on a simple recognition. The fundamental parameters governing the outlook for humanity's future in terms of energy, war, water, food, and population are hopeful. We examine them in the chapters to come and conclude that within these objective boundaries economic, security, and social policies can lead to a peaceful and stable world that works better than today.

But we believe that many of these policies will not be implemented as long as the expectation of nuclear devastation, global or local, remains as high as it is today. The end of the nuclear arms race and the cuts in nuclear arsenals resulting from the Strategic Arms Reductions treaties (START I and II) and the Intermediate Nuclear Forces Treaty have reduced, but by no means eliminated, the expectation of nuclear catastrophe. Some 20,000 nuclear weapons are still usable. It is not prudent for governments of nations, nuclear and nonnuclear, to ignore that fact, and most of them don't. There are two possible approaches to this problem: continuing military preparedness and preparations to deter a nuclear attack, or genuine and persistent efforts to eliminate operational nuclear arsenals and, until this is achieved, efforts to dampen the demand for nuclear weapons.

When in wartime (1943) Niels Bohr came first to Los Alamos, he asked Robert Oppenheimer one question: is the atomic bomb big enough? By that he meant to open a chilling question: would the threat posed by the bomb be enough to reform the international order? Oppenheimer would much later recall his own thinking. "I don't know if it was big enough then," he said, "but it got to be."[9] It seems that we are witnesses to that eventual truth, able now to assess a world stock that ran to 40 or 50 *thousand* ready nuclear weapons, a stock now cut by half.[10]

If the threat of large-scale nuclear war is receding, we can ascribe that change (if our arguments hold merit) partly to the rational if largely implicit calculation of its inordinate danger, one unprecedented for populations in the Northern Hemisphere, its risks fully shared by leaders and simple citizens alike. The bomb had indeed gotten big enough to matter a great deal.

Irony

Here ironically is reason to hope indeed, because some sort of reasoned behavior prevailed in these last fifty years, when the powers built—*but never used*—their expensive weapons of mutual and thorough self-destruction, a true threat to the entire gain in the expected length of life achieved since the rise of steam power in the Atlantic world. Those powers drew back, and the people survived.

How much the bald demographic facts of this chapter can affect events we cannot say. They distill both the perils of nuclear destruction and the instabilities that accompany the sharp demographic transition, both unique in human history. We see no better path to alleviating the calamities of pestilence, war, and famine than a reasoned, persistent effort to organize nations against them, first against large-scale nuclear war, and then against the smaller wars by reducing the illusion of gain. Those lesser wars will not alter the evolution of the demographic transition, but they rob humanity of resources and opportunity to deal with the many problems the transition entrains.

Certainly courage, selfless devotion, pride, and high challenge to leadership are as evident in war as are their opposites, hate, fear, greed, and the call for vengeance. Those contradictory displays are commonplaces of history. Human virtues do not suffice for peace, even though they are as necessary for peace as for war. We need not wait for virtues alone, but we can hope that nations newly organized to act together will come to follow new paths along a curve of learning. No new order will bring perfection, or even an unbroken peace, but step by step we can restore our future.

3

U.S. Nuclear Forces for the Next Century

Twenty-four hours a day in every season, unfailingly for thirty years without a break, one or another of a carefully tended group of specially equipped big jets was somewhere aloft, high over North America or the seas adjoining. Within that far-off plane on its determinedly random track a dozen or two technicians attended the panels and screens of secure long-range communications. The chosen few, a general officer of the U.S. Strategic Air Command and his staff, endured the long hours airborne until word should come that the next plane and crew in the unceasing rotation had safely taken off. Only upon confirmed replacement could the tired crew members return to a SAC runway, so that after a few days they might again take up their place in perpetual vigil aloft.

That was Looking Glass, an airborne surrogate command post.[1] Should the White House, the Pentagon, and the buried center of SAC at Omaha be destroyed or isolated by a sudden nuclear strike, the grave and anonymous officers of Looking Glass, prepared by long training and strict orders, would send the same coded commands their vanished president might have used to loose the awesome retaliation of the United States. Such provision for catastrophic strike-back even in extremis would, it was held, deter the initial vaporizing attack: mutual destruction was assured.

Looking Glass first took up its unending rounds in February 1961. SAC ended its anxious, ceaseless, airborne rotation in July 1991. The thread of thermonuclear confrontation is no longer drawn taut, a surcease widely felt.

With the credibility of communist expansion ended, this nation can return to a condign level of military preparedness and the traditional economic basis of security. The debate goes on: how fast can such reductions take place, how far should they go, and when to begin in earnest?

U.S. forces now need to reflect the real armed world and its risks, not the shadowy image we once anxiously watched in the mirror. How much military force is enough? That balance must be reckoned afresh, starting with the huge inventory of weapons and our large contingent of trained forces. Certainly prudence implies that change cannot be too sudden, nor go beyond all possibility of reversal. Nevertheless we propose that U.S. defenses be steadily and sharply reduced, both the nuclear weaponry, so terrible but so cheap, and the grand panoply of expensive hardware we call conventional: planes, ships, tanks, and missiles. Of the close to 4 million men and women, in uniform and out, who now build, organize, and bear American arms, most will need to be set new constructive tasks in the next decade.

To arrive at adequate yet affordable long-term military preparations, policymakers need a yardstick. What is enough nuclear and conventional power depends on what missions and functions the political leadership expects our military to perform successfully ten or more years from now. It is quite improbable, for instance, that the United States will become involved in a land war with nuclear-armed China. We therefore do not need in peacetime to match the size of the largest army in the world, the one mustered by China, the most populous nation. Indeed, the United States has not done so since Western allies marched to Peking in 1900, though we have since fought the fraction of Chinese armies sent into Korea.

The normative assumption we make here is that the United States will retain strong nuclear deterrent forces to avoid but not to initiate nuclear war, and keep enough nonnuclear forces to deter and even prevail in any theater of war where the country could plausibly find itself at war alone, without well-armed allies. These assured aims imply a large decrease in our conventional forces. We thus begin with a clear requirement—firm deterrence against future threats of nuclear war, and drastic reductions of nuclear arsenals. (We defer our analysis of conventional forces to chapter 7.)

The primacy of this requirement derives from the millionfold greater destructive capacity of nuclear explosives, capable not just of reducing the life expectancy of the population of a nation by a year or so, as did conventional weapons during the cruelest wars half a century ago, but also of snuffing out entire organized societies.

Nuclear Deterrence

While concepts like military superiority and the victory in combat that it anticipates may still decide the calculus of adequate conventional arsenals, they have ceased informing nuclear policy since 1950. Combat between two conventionally armed opponents may create a winner and a loser: an asymmetrical outcome. Thereby the conflict is resolved, at least for a time. But nuclear combat between two strong nuclear weapons states will always end with both combatants sustaining a mirrored devastation. A few hundred delivered nuclear explosives can therefore deter, for they assure symmetrical obliteration of the major urban and industrial centers even of the largest countries, such as Russia and the United States. Beyond some modest number of nuclear weapons, their marginal destructiveness rapidly approaches zero: the value of the targets that remain has simply fallen too low.

Nuclear deterrence remains today as it was before, assigned to the missile silos, submarine missile launchers, and long-reach bomber aircraft, all three integrated to assure appropriate retaliation to any nuclear attack: the familiar Triad. Strategic nuclear weapons are meant to destroy enemy homeland targets, military or civilian, at any distance. Their use in warfare has steadily lost credibility. In June 1991, just prior to the great changes in Moscow, our American forces deployed not just 100 or even 1,000 but about 9,750 warheads on strategic nuclear weapons, many having a yield a hundred times larger than the nuclear bombs of World War II.[2] The overkill was authentic indeed.

The eventual elimination of all these weapons of mass destruction is the claimed goal of the leaders of most nuclear-armed lands. The possibility of small surreptitious stocks of nuclear weapons, and the need to deter reckless leaders or those attracted by the mythic attributes of destructive power, suggest that no quick elimination of all nuclear weapons is ahead. Certainly the nuclear powers have been slow to move toward that goal. Moreover, in spite of the legalities, all sovereign states are simply not in fact equal. The powerful have established power to coerce the weak, and the former are not apt to relinquish that power lightly.

The Strategic Arms Reduction Treaty (START I), signed in Moscow in July 1991 and ratified in 1994, imposes a variety of numerical limits on nuclear arms, verified on the spot, and routinely monitored, all to be reached before 2000.[3] It is plainly in the spirit of the times to go further, as indeed Presidents Bush and Yeltsin did with START II in 1993. We propose that U.S. nuclear forces undergo additional sharp cuts to bring them well below the levels of START I and START II, ratified by the U.S. Senate in 1996, but not yet by Russia (as of early 1998).

Let us be candid: the forces we suggest here for the decades beyond the year 2000 are not sized by concern for long-term world safety and good sense within an enduring international regime, but stem from our judgment that caution still governs the national will; profound changes can come only slowly. The force levels we suggest can still disassemble the economy and society of a large nation like the United States or Russia, and so can be recognized even by worst-case adherents as an assured deterrent to nuclear attack.

Adequate U.S. Nuclear Forces for the Next Century

Both before and especially after the end of the Cold War it was widely accepted that the loss of ten cities caused by a retaliatory nuclear attack would be a political, economic, and human disaster enough to deter any U.S. or Soviet government from starting a nuclear war. By this minimal calculus a mere dozen assuredly deliverable megaton-size nuclear explosives would compose an adequate arsenal. (By the same calculus, it is not just a large-scale nuclear war that concerns us but the accidental engagement in a nuclear exchange that involves a few dozen warheads.) Given the possibility of a preemptive strike that could erode one's retaliatory force, and given operational and deployment vagaries, an arsenal of two-score weapons would be likely to deter any nuclear aggressor. Yet the price of a miscalculation of what would deter an opponent is so vast that one must be most conservative in setting the level of damage that can deter beyond doubt.

How easily a modest number of nuclear weapons, hundreds rather than thousands, could demolish the national economy of a large and powerful country and therefore constitute an unquestionable deterrent, is demonstrated by a hypothetical analysis simulating one specialized attack. The plan entails denying just one technology—the economic use of liquid hydrocarbons—to one nation, our own wide United States, so deeply dependent on that technology.

Such a counter-energy attack might consist of 85 550-kiloton weapons and 154 200-kiloton weapons, a total of 239 nuclear warheads adding up to less than 2 percent of the equivalent megatonnage the Soviet Union deployed in 1986. The attack scenario examined here is designed to inflict the maximum *economic* damage while minimizing the attack size. All the same, about 20 million Americans would die immediately as a result of this attack, which also injures 5 million: casualties total 10 percent of the entire population.

Since all U.S. wars combined have taken less than 2 million American lives, since the worst of our epidemics took a million or so, the threat of such loss under "modest" attack seems utterly deterring, the more since most damage would be done over a matter of days, if not hours. In all, in this attack the United States loses 33 percent of its capacity to produce energy, 19 percent of its capacity to make metals, and between 5 and 10 percent of its capacity to manufacture other products; overall, the U.S. economy would lose only 8 percent of its total manufacturing capacity. Such a limited attack, from just 1 percent of the Soviet Union's nuclear arsenal during the 1980s, would devastate the U.S. economy because it would first deny this country 98 percent of all transportation fuel. Foreign refining facilities can only supply a small part of the production destroyed. And foreign imports might be almost completely cut off for an extended period of time by parallel destruction of commercial ports, especially since bulk oil requires elaborate import facilities. Improvisation of refineries and emergency use of wood, coal, and so on could enable the transport of only a fraction of the huge output of farm and factory. Nationwide transportation would come to a halt.

In fact, we must imagine the United States without appreciable transportation for at least several months. After that it would remain cut severely, able to supply the bare essentials but not restored fully for as long as several years. One special danger of the swift drastic shortfall in petroleum is that it would cut off access to existing fuel supplies in oil fields and coal mines. Fuel is needed to extract and transport fuel. Thus a nation has a minimum energy requirement, an *energy threshold.*

As a consequence of the absence not of agricultural products themselves but of *transportation* for agricultural products, far more people would die of famine during the first two years after the attack (about 50 percent) than would be killed by the attack itself (about 10 percent). Urban starvation in the second and third years after the attack—evacuation of the cities would be arduous, especially in the Northeast—as a direct result of the lack of transportation would be unavoidable.

Even if the improvisations and abrupt changes in citizen behavior— tight rationing, long refugee movements, and much more—make these broadly economic inferences uncertain, it is hard to see that the attack could do less than return many regions of our country to a state resembling the TV images of Somalia in 1991. At worst, a modest nuclear attack can induce a permanent collapse in the U.S. economy, even though no nuclear explosions occur in almost half of the fifty states! At the least it would induce stagnation and a much reduced standard of living for years for a major fraction of a pauperized nation, mourning more of our dead than in all the wars of this Republic.

Such damage is unacceptable to any sane political leadership. The outcome makes clear that broadly destroying the socioeconomic fabric of a nation, even a land as large, diverse, and prosperous as the United States, using nuclear weapons by hundreds (less than 10 percent of our drastically *reduced* post–Cold War arsenals) would be physically easy.

Even the folly of preemption, the first strike, cannot protect against nuclear economic devastation. Neither can defense. Nuclear weapons can be carried to their targets by ships, by aircraft, by cruise and ballistic missiles, even stealthily within ordinary commerce. Unlike ordinary explosives that required thousands of sorties to inflict damage to German urban and industrial centers during World War II, a single nuclear weapon can devastate a city; 200 of them threaten collapse to a country the size of the United States. Given the structure of the Russian industry and urban habitat, an even smaller number could have similar economic and social effects. This simple imperative imposes decisive conclusions regarding nuclear policy of our nation.

We judge then that at any time during the Cold War some 200 assuredly deliverable nuclear explosives constituted credible deterrence against the aggressor at its most sanguine. Since, however, such an aggressor could have attacked the deterring arsenal of its opponent in a surprise attack, the actual peacetime size of the deterring arsenal would have to be some small multiple of 200 explosives. Our proposed U.S. nuclear arsenal for the first decade of the next century is based on this cautious calculus.

Reducing Our Present Nuclear Forces

We take up one by one the different U.S. nuclear weapons systems now in place.

Land-Based Ballistic Missiles

Eliminating all but a single warhead in each land-based missile ends the main incentive for preemptive attack on the easily located and immobile silos: one warhead is spent to destroy at best only one warhead, and some of them will miss.[4] The stated intention of the U.S. Department of Defense is to maintain current numbers (500) of the present Minuteman IIIs, but with single-warhead loading. The smaller force of Minutemen that we propose—300—is quite adequate for deterrence.

Ballistic-Missile Submarines

We would keep only the ten newest missile submarines, some still to be built, all able to patrol safely far offshore. But we propose just a single warhead instead of eight in each of the twenty-four missiles aboard an Ohio-class submarine. We would arrange the rotation of subs and crews to maintain six of the ten vessels always safe on sea patrol—about the number that patrol today.

Strategic Nuclear Bombers

A bomber brings commander and crew close to the target, into harm's way, where danger and admiration alike have dwelt since war began. These "slow" air-breathing, vulnerable aircraft need hours to reach any target, not the half-hour that an orbiting missile takes. Therefore the decision to strike can be reconsidered for some time after takeoff, and airborne crews even have time for judgment. To be sure, a modern compromise has been struck with the old image of heroic piloted penetration deep into enemy territory: the bombing crew may choose to carry gravity bombs all the way in, or to launch small ballistic missiles from a couple of hundred miles away, or to send out long-range cruise missiles that may not even require the bomber to cross an enemy border. The mix of bomber payloads is easily chosen mission by mission.

START I rules counting nuclear weapons on both sides favor the aircraft mode of delivery, since bombers are believed unlikely weapons for a first strike. We are left unconvinced by this special pleading. Why augment the nuclear bomber force, vulnerable on the runways, expensive if kept aloft, and unlikely to find deterrent use? But since we seek to avoid too rapid change in the traditional rationale for placing one's dragon's eggs into many baskets, we accept some bombers, only the least costly and the least provocative ones—the older B-52s, armed with existing "standoff" weapons, which can be launched from some distance from the target without loss of accuracy. We propose to deploy no nuclear-armed "stealthy" B-2s (the 1993 budget contracted for twenty of them) and no new advanced cruise missiles. The B-2 aircraft are acclaimed by their friends for their speed and low visibility to waiting radars. But they have more than a few technical flaws not easily remedied, and a dauntingly high cost. And despite their stealth, radar picks them up, though at reduced range—perhaps no shorter than half of the usual early warning distance.

Overall, a number of airborne warheads comparable to that of the other two arms of the Triad would seem quite enough. Why should the rubble bounce?

Tactical Nuclear Weapons

Tactical weapons, often of smaller energy yield, are meant for battlefield use against engaged combat forces or their forward support—the airfields, bases, and transportation nodes as far as a few hundred miles behind the lines. (They were not wholly wrong who coined the cynical definition that a tactical nuclear weapon was one intended to explode within Germany.) One cannot overlook the view that we deployed such weapons in part to placate the European desire for more U.S. troops in Europe as visible guarantors of our pledged engagement. It is not necessary to use much space to explain the decline of interest in tactical nuclear weapons now that Germany is reunited.

In September 1991 President Bush wisely ordered the elimination of nearly all U.S. sea- or land-launched tactical nuclear weapons. At sea only the carrier-based attack bombers of longer range (mainly Grumman A-6 Intruders) remain afloat, fewer than 50 bombs on each active carrier, by our estimate 600 or 700 in total. Such shipboard capacity to initiate nuclear war against even nonnuclear states is hardly tolerable, and even dangerous. We recommend that all these weapons be set ashore and dismantled before the year 2000.

There is little military purpose for the nearly 1,000 nuclear gravity bombs we estimate the United States still deploys on offshore lands. But there are sharp diplomatic issues: France and Britain have comparable arms in Europe in similar numbers. We recommend that allied negotiations to end all deployment of tactical nuclear weapons in Europe get under way at once, with the participation of Germany and states to the east as acutely interested participants. We would wager that all states involved will in fact agree on ending this ugly danger. Pending such agreement we propose to immediately reduce our own tactical deployment to about 250 gravity bombs on U.S. tactical aircraft in Europe.

Strategic Defenses

A modest defense of U.S. territory against bomber aircraft and planes carrying cruise missiles is now assigned to 160 modern fighter-interceptors of the Air National Guard, joined by about 50 Canadian fighters.[5] Their joint watch oversees the Arctic approaches, where an automated radar net, the North Warning System, is newly in service. Defense against long-range ballistic missiles is still planned. That defense can do nothing against covert nuclear attack, itself unlikely though rather more likely than a few missiles conspicuously sent into orbit our way by some highly targetable—and suicidal—leader. We recommend continued study of antimissile systems but not large amounts of money developing them, cutting annual funding to about $1 billion for R&D.

The elaborate and indispensable systems in orbit that connect our forces, guide them, and warn of nuclear attack are so thoroughly useful for conventional war as well that we will treat them within that wider context in chapter 7.

Making Nuclear Weapons

The chief military expenditure of the United States that does not appear in the annual budget of the Department of Defense is the cost of building new nuclear weapons, or reworking old ones into new. Nuclear weapons manufacture, research, and testing are all included among the military tasks of the Department of Energy. The continuation of underground testing after more than a thousand U.S. tests on the record attested to our long stance of anxious readiness more than a technical need. Tests have now stopped by a treaty signed in 1996 but not yet ratified by the U.S. Senate; the signal they send to aspirant nuclear powers was a real source of danger.

The U.S. production of weapons and nuclear explosives, including tests and the reprocessing of nuclear warship fuel, costs about $8 billion, expended in some sixteen specialized (and often contaminated) plants over a dozen states. Three large DOE labs perform design, development, engineering, and testing. Plainly these activities will drop sharply, while disassembly of weapons for storage or disposal, all carried done at the Pantex plant in Amarillo, Texas, will as sharply increase. Even now Pantex is working solely on disassembly; no new warheads are now in production. Meticulous and highly technical attention is needed all through the dangerous journey from silo to safe disposal.

The three bomb labs should be condensed to two, Los Alamos and Sandia, both in New Mexico; the lab in Livermore, California, could continue doing civilian energy work alone. The costs of various control, surveillance, and safety activities would remain. We estimate that, given the weapons reductions outline above, these can cost some $2 billion annually. (This does not include the costs of cleaning up contaminated DOE bomb-making facilities and nuclear waste.)

By now-familiar calculations, a U.S. arsenal that consisted of 300 single-warhead intercontinental ballistic missiles (ICBMs) protected in hard silos, 240 nuclear warheads deployed on 10 submarines, and 50 bombers each carrying 2 nuclear bombs would still contain about 240 deliverable weapons after a surprise peak Russian attack (hardly plausible today from a disordered Russian force). Conversely, about 160 Russian weapons would survive a U.S. surprise attack on a similar Russian nuclear arsenal. (The difference between the two outcomes is due to the larger fraction of Soviet submarines held in port at any one time and the greater accuracy of U.S.

countersilo warheads. Arsenals consisting of 480 nuclear explosives exclusively deployed on submarines, which can move about the oceans undetected, would be even more secure.) The latter U.S. arsenal would still contain over 300 warheads after a surprise attack against it, and the corresponding Russian arsenal a few less than 200. The Russians could improve the survivability of their submarine force by having a larger fraction of their ballistic missile-carrying subs out in the ocean at all times, an easy upgrade. Several other combinations of silo-based ICBMs, submarine-based ballistic missiles, and bombers could ensure similar survivable fractions. We conclude then that an arsenal of about 700 nuclear weapons would have provided unquestionably assured deterrence against nuclear attack to both the United States and the Soviet Union during the Cold War. Many fewer nuclear weapons can achieve this imperative in the temperate political climate of the post-Cold War era.

We tabulate in table 3.1 the nuclear forces that we propose the United States should deploy until the early years of the next decade, in the spirit of the Bush-Yeltsin agreement of January 1993. The 1993 treaty fixes a rough parity between the parties, but at a level that can threaten survival on Earth if the arsenals are used. The cut we propose in U.S. overkill is large and long overdue, yet it leaves all three legs of the Triad forceful indeed.

Table 3.1
Proposed U.S. nuclear forces (count by warheads)

	Bush-Yeltsin for 2003	Our proposal for beyond
Land-based ballistic missiles	500	300
Undersea ballistic missiles	1,728	240
Bombers	1,272	240
Total strategic warheads	**3,500**	**780**
Tactical nuclear warheads	1,600	250

Source: *Annual Report of the Secretary of Defense to the President and the Congress,* 1996, pp. 213–214 and app. D–1.
Notes: (1) The land-based missiles are single-warhead Minuteman IIIs. (2) In the Bush-Yeltsin agreement, the U.S. holds undersea missiles on 18 Trident subs in 432 tubes; our proposal is for 10 Tridents with single-warhead missiles in 240 tubes. (3) Bush-Yeltsin proposes 20 B-2s and 100 B-52Hs; our suggested total is 60 B-52H aircraft.

The proposed Russian forces total about 500 warheads based on land, 1,700 based undersea, plus 60 slow Bear-H bombers, nominally loaded with 750 warheads. These numbers are not very likely to become ready deployments.

Even when moderated, U.S. nuclear power would still be awful, a cruel threat of unprecedented mass destruction; surely this country and humanity can do better. The taking of whole nations hostage must one day end, but we do not foresee its ending soon. Yet a prompt reduction is an essential and an urgent step against the proliferation of nuclear weapons worldwide, a growing concern for long-term policy.

The costs of the nuclear arsenal discussed above can be calculated. The costs vary widely according to the assumptions one allows. In the mixed arsenal of 300 single-warhead silo-based ICBMs, 240 submarine-based warheads, and 240 air-launched cruise missiles, the cost of research, acquisition, and 15 years' worth of operations and maintenance, plus the pro-rated cost per warhead of the aircraft, missile, or submarine that would carry each weapon, comes to $50 million per silo-based warhead, $44 million per submarine-based warhead, and $65 million per bomber-carried bomb or warhead, for a total arsenal cost of $40.6 billion. For a solely submarine-based deterrent of 480 warheads, the cost would be $21.0 billion. A more relevant calculation of expenditures may be the cost of each *surviving* weapon after a preemptive attack against the U.S. deterrent arsenal. If we assume that circumstances favored the attacker, and the attack came by surprise, the cost of each surviving weapon would be at its maximum; while if the attack favored the victim (in this case the United States), and there was a 72-hour warning, then the cost of each surviving warhead would be at its minimum.

Under all circumstances an all-sea-based retaliatory force would be the most cost effective. The cost of maintaining and operating this 780-warhead strategic nuclear arsenal, weapons facilities, and personnel amounts to about $15 billion per year.

Deterrence and the need to maintain a nuclear arsenal in order to implement it implies hostile intent between two or more nations. It would be logical to assume, then, that now that the state of hostility between the United States and the nuclear states of the former Soviet Union has ceased, now that the threat of a nuclear attack has evaporated, nuclear arsenals would also disappear. But just as the number of nuclear explosives in the arsenals of the two nuclear giants was not proportional to the threat each posed to the other, so now the reduction of the nuclear arsenals is not proportional to the decreasing nuclear threat. We are witnessing a hysteresis in leadership, and even in public opinion, very similar to the magnetic hysteresis electrical engineers are familiar with; proper response lags the actual ending of the stimulus. At the beginning of the arms race, the number of nuclear weapons in the United States increased more or less proportionately to the perceived threat from the Stalinist Soviet Union. Thereafter, even though the threat varied little, U.S. and Soviet arsenals increased explosively to tens of thousands of warheads, until saturation set in. Special cooperative efforts will be needed to move beyond arsenals measured in the thousands, as seems prudent for the long run.

World Nuclear Weapons

For comparison we tabulate in table 3.2 the nuclear holdings of the first five overt nuclear powers.

These numbers will decline considerably over the next few years. The Bush-Yeltsin agreement signed in 1992 limits the United States to 3,500 and Russia to 3,000 warheads by 2002. The Chinese force contains no

Table 3.2
Strategic nuclear weapons (weapons with transoceanic reach) in the original declared five nuclear powers, 1996

	United States	Former Soviet Union	United Kingdom	France	China
ICBMS	575	727	—	18	7
Warheads	2,075	3,750	—	18	7
Submarines	17	27	4	4	2
Missiles	408	440	—	64	12
Warheads	3,264	2,350	94–128	380	12
Bombers	179	70	150	60	150
Bombs and missiles	1,800	1,400	~200	24	150
Total warheads	~7,800	~7,500	~320	426	~200

Source: William Arkin, "Nuclear Notebook," *Bulletin of the Atomic Scientists* July/August 1996, p. 63; September/October 1996, p. 63; November/December 1996, pp. 64–67.

more than a few dozen true ICBMs; the rest of their missiles are of intermediate range.

We also tabulate the plausible holdings and visible nuclear policies of other nuclear-capable states. The discussion of the state of nuclear weapons outside the five can deceive no one; clearly this compilation (table 3.3) is at best a rough and uncertain guide to what is ahead, for it is an explicit mix of evidence, rumor, surmise, and leaked information.

Table 3.3
Other nuclear nations beyond the original five

Israel	No test but has 50–100 nearly ready warheads. Its delivery vehicles are jet fighter-bombers and intermediate-range ballistic missiles. The situation we ascribe to Israel is widely believed, though the confirmation is uncertain.
India	Made a second series of nuclear tests in 1998; has 50–80 bombs and warheads. Delivery vehicles: jet fighter-bombers; Intermediate-Range Ballistic Missiles under development
Pakistan	Tested in 1998 and is believed to have perhaps 10–20 warheads. These may be of a tested foreign design. Delivery vehicles: jet fighter-bombers.
South Africa	Has worked on bombs during the late 1970s. Made 6 or more Hiroshima-type bombs. Abandoned the effort in 1990 and declared that it will dismantle the weapons.
North Korea	Reported to be in late stages of warhead fabrication. Has decided to abandon its current nuclear efforts.
Iraq	Postwar UN inspection reported that Iraq was well along in development. Possible delivery by aircraft and short-range missiles.
Libya, Syria, perhaps Iran, Algeria	Long interested in acquiring nuclear weapons.
Argentina, Brazil, Sweden	Took steps to develop nuclear weapons, then stopped on their own.
Germany, Italy, Japan, Switzerland, Sweden, perhaps Taiwan	Able to produce nuclear warheads within a year or so after a decision

Note: The numbers and details of these forces have been drawn from widespread but unconfirmed intelligence reports. They are measures of the general state of nuclearization of these countries rather than exact descriptions of their arsenals.

Less clear is whether we can rely roughly on all these estimates. We differentiate among the five. The superpowers, the former Soviet forces and the U.S. forces, have been so long and deeply linked in adversarial surveillance that we believe the published reports are broadly accurate. Such large arsenals are not likely to be much affected by any decision to keep secret a fraction of the holdings. (If anything, both sides had some reason to overstate their prowess.) The much smaller forces of France and the United Kingdom have been closely coupled to U.S. technology over the years. We doubt that those states have any substantial forces hidden, the more because parliamentary control has been present even through policy change.

The Chinese forces, for three decades the least connected with the outside world, are not so easily understood. That power has neither a substantial undersea force nor any large ICBM force it can rapidly and assuredly fire. China has at least a plausible motive and the ability to conceal some substantial retaliatory force. Their production infrastructure is large enough to have produced rather more than the deployed weapons reported and accepted under international intelligence consensus. We would not be astonished if the ample tunnels in the mountainous Chinese northwest houses some backup nuclear delivery systems in addition to the diverse military assets for which they were built. Even concealment within military-industrial complexes rural and urban is possible. A hidden force, although slow to respond to attack, cannot be held unlikely, and rumors to that effect even circulate. But no change in order of magnitude would go undetected, and a Chinese effort to project uncertainty about whether it can launch a retaliatory strike is not destabilizing in their strategic situation.

A gloomy and little-discussed topic is the possibility that a nuclear state would place some nuclear weapons in alien territory as a hedge against an attack by that adversary. Any technically capable state could do that either by exporting some weapons clandestinely to foreign capitals or by emplacing thermonuclear sea mines offshore from coastal cities, which would become targets for tidal waves. There is no sign of any such hazards. But it is clear that political, diplomatic, and on-site technical assurances that preclude such activities will need to be worked out before the five will be ready to reduce their weapons holdings to eventual small limits near zero.

Beyond 2000: Proliferation and Opportunity

We cannot claim to be prophets. The long term is not visible in detail. Certainly the old idea of unending military superiority has proven inadequate to keep us out of mortal danger, even if mutual prudence kept away the nuclear catastrophe that mediated our interactions with the Soviet Union. The spread of technology and trade is not likely to stop; with it comes the increasing risk of multiple proliferation of weapons of mass destruction. It is our view that no other foreseeable weapons system in the technological future rivals the inherent danger of nuclear weapons. Neither biological nor chemical weapons seem decisive against prepared adversaries. The international regimes that regulate both the chemical and biological weapons that now exist and those under active preparation reflect that wide consensus.

We all sense that a world of anxious nuclear powers—nations with a mindset like ours for four decades—is less than stable, especially for peoples in the underdeveloped nations. We will not avoid that world solely by prohibiting supply, even with clever and determined policing. The demand side will need to be faced, above all by a wider international sharing both of hope and of decision. The fragile atmosphere of Earth is held in common; neither the physical climate nor the moral one can forever survive the unlimited potential for damage posed by the nuclear arsenals deployed today.

That no victory lies in nuclear exchange has kept the nuclear powers at the brink for the past half-century, but never beyond it. Yet there remain circumstances in which the use of nuclear explosives is thinkable. Hiroshima and Nagasaki illustrated early the first instance: only one side possesses nuclear weapons. Another instance is when only one side is targetable; a parastatal, poorly localized holder of a few nuclear explosives might use them because that holder is untargetable, perhaps not even identifiable. One-sided possession of nuclear explosives confers military advantage. With sharp binary asymmetry between the nuclear haves and have-nots, nuclear weapons can be—and have been—instruments of tacit coercion by the haves against the have-nots. In this context efforts to prevent nuclear proliferation by denying the means for producing weapons can be and have been viewed as a form of "nuclear imperialism"; some have-nots even regard nuclear weapons as an urgent human right! The fear of nuclear asymmetry has been the strongest motive for nuclear possession. Stalin feared the U.S. nuclear monopoly; and Chinese leaders, the Soviet bombs. India found nuclear asymmetry with China intolerable, tested a bomb once, and now has a nuclear stockpile, probably with a score of weapons. Pakistan has responded in turn to the pattern of local nuclear threat and has tested some weapons (probably of imported design). Both India and Pakistan held their weapons until 1998 as undeployed deterrents. This cautious approach was not without its high cost. Nuclear competition among proliferating states causes local instabilities and virulent arms races that detract from efforts to improve life and deal with problems spawned by demographic transition and environmental degradation. Logic would argue that once nuclear-capable, a nation should relax its military vigilance, secure behind its nuclear armamentarium. Yet, with the possible exception of China, nations possessing nuclear weapons, or even aspiring to such possession, have continued their arms race in conventional weapons.

Nuclear asymmetry is occasionally sought to counterbalance another strong asymmetry of power. Israel pursued and amassed its nuclear arsenal to counter the large asymmetry in population and in maneuvering space between it and its larger Arab neighbors. That same population asymmetry urged white South Africans toward nuclear possession. The Republic of South Africa worked on nuclear warheads during the 1970s; it has abandoned that work and signed the Nuclear Non-Proliferation Treaty. For the developed "North," nuclear asymmetry with the vastly more populous South may be seen by some as an ultimate unheralded insurance against some future forceful reduction of the economic asymmetry between the two.

When nuclear asymmetry is not seen as a mortal danger, even states that could develop nuclear weapons have not done so. Italy, Sweden, Switzerland, Germany, and Japan, all with the scientific know-how and industrial infrastructure for production of nuclear weapons, have chosen so far to remain outside the nuclear club. (Sweden actually began its development but soon laid it aside.) Germany and Japan maintain constitutional bans against the possession of nuclear weapons. Along with the NATO states besides Germany, they are somewhat protected against nuclear attack by assurances of American action against any nuclear aggressor.

Nuclear self-denial by a mutual recent agreement between Argentina and Brazil illustrates the effectiveness of still another inhibitor to nuclear possession. While nuclear weapons are relatively cheap to acquire, they are not free. They imply enormous costs if they lead to high anxieties among neighbors. The economic rewards of mutual abstinence are evident.

Scientific and technological capabilities have spread slowly but surely to newly industrializing states worldwide. Iraq is only the case at hand, its arming well managed and well financed, but consider the early examples of nuclear-armed China and nuclear-capable India as well. That Israel is nuclear-armed is a half-open secret; it holds an estimated 50 to 100 warheads. All three nations were assisted along the path by foreign aid. The two Koreas and Taiwan might become candidate-members of the nuclear club as their technical prowess grows. Iran appears able to emulate its belligerent neighbor Iraq, and Algeria might start along the path too, as Libya has tried mainly by purchase.

It is far better for international nonproliferation efforts to recognize that supply responds to demand, that intention precedes capability. Honest attention to the demand side should become a strong complement to the supply-side efforts of the United States in nuclear nonproliferation. A serious approach to a universal pledge against the use of nuclear weapons against nonnuclear states makes a beginning on the juridical plane. One day that will extend to physical measures, further reductions in weapons stockpiles, the monitored end of nuclear tests by all nuclear states, and the end of new weapons fabrication in all states. Then finally, even nuclear weapons deployment can be ended. All these measures tend to reduce the appeal of these weapons to other nations.

In December 1996, a group of some sixty senior military officers from sixteen countries, more than half from the United States, Russia, the United Kingdom, France, and India, issued an unprecedented public appeal to Presidents Clinton and Yeltsin: "Reduce, Take Off Alert, Abolish." They called for a steady, phased cooperative plan "reducing nuclear weapons step by step to the lowest verifiable levels consistent with stable security, as rapidly as world conditions permit . . . The time for action is now." They remark of nuclear weapons: "They are not needed against nonnuclear opponents. Conventional capabilities can provide a sufficient deterrent and defense against conventional forces and the threat of chemical and biological weapons. As symbols of prestige and standing, nuclear weapons are of markedly reduced importance."

The leader of this group was General George L. Butler, former commander-in-chief, U.S. Strategic Air Command (1991–92), then commander-in-chief, U.S. Strategic Command (1992–94), responsible for all U.S. strategic nuclear forces, air, land, sea, and space. He was seconded by General Andrew Goodpaster (retired), former supreme allied commander in Europe (1969–74), after long service under General and President Eisenhower. Apparently this public statement grew out of discussion among a group assembled in Canberra in 1995 under the auspices of the government of Australia. We cannot fail to look upon this juncture as a hopeful sign that may in the end modify the stance of governments. The statement is not without still earlier roots; anyone acquainted with reflective people in military service has good reason to know that many of them concur with what these commanders say.

As the United States and its allies prepared to drive Iraqi ground forces from Kuwait in 1991, President Bush declared that the United States would not hesitate to take whatever action was necessary to retaliate against any use of chemical weapons against American troops. This was widely read as a warning that the United States might use nuclear weapons in such a contingency. Even more troubling is the recent echo of this idea from the 1997 White House, directed not against a barrage of toxic Scuds, but intended to pull mutinous senators into line. They were promised a similar White House warning of such "extended nuclear deterrence" if they would abate their opposition to ratification of the pending Convention on Chemical Warfare. Again, the voices of seasoned commanders are less bellicose than the sallies of political infighters.

Our coastal cities are more vulnerable to easily smuggled covert nukes than to uncertain efforts at long-range biological or chemical attack by second-string enemies far away. It goes without saying that a policy of "extended deterrence" enhances any poor man's interest in a few nuclear weapons. That is a dangerous setback to the safety of our powerful country in the long run, as indeed for every other nuclear state. Our nuclear overkill remains, and as the world changes around us, we are threatening ourselves more and more each day.

All our specifically nuclear forces—though able to devastate whole continents in a day's time—now account for under one-fifth of the total U.S. military expenditure. More than 80 cents of every military dollar go to pay for our conventional forces.[6] (The capacity for nuclear destruction has become so terrible in part because its means are so cheap to procure.) The nonnuclear forces are of decisive significance to U.S. military posture. In chapter 7 we will analyze conventional force needs, summing up the dollar costs of those proposed smaller forces and of smaller U.S. nuclear forces as well, looking both short term and some decades into the next century.

4

Mending the Leaks in Nonproliferation

Preventing wider proliferation of nuclear weapons beyond the aging Club of Five seems newly urgent these days. The Security Council has learned how much the Non-Proliferation Treaty leaked beside the Euphrates; the subcontinent of India has now reached a "postproliferation stage." Hope for safe arrival in a world without many more nuclear powers is slowly fading.

The proliferation of sophisticated weapons like supersonic jet fighters around the world during the Cold War years was seen as an unavoidable symptom of the overarching East-West confrontation. Whether by sale or by concessionary forms of transfer, weapons, though not nuclear weapons, were a handy currency of support for nations on "our side," and often vehicles of foreign policy. Yet the collapse of the Soviet Union has lessened but not eliminated weapons proliferation. On the contrary, 1993 was a banner year[1] for weapons exports to less-developed countries, although sales have since fallen. Governments and industry of the developed North see in those exports profit, industrial jobs, and sharing of the capital costs now sunk into weapons development. The supply readily responds to a rising demand that owes a good deal to the prowess of high-tech weapons in the brief Gulf War.

Weapons trade is one route of weapons proliferation in the developing world; indigenous production is the second. The latter is a costlier, chancier path, but a wide-open one, difficult to block by external barriers and controls and steadily eased by the gradual growth in scientific and technological expertise in every rapidly industrializing nation. Proliferation of advanced weapons through indigenous production, often in reaction to efforts by the North to deny supply, suggests no easily grasped solutions.

Denial of relevant technology can eventually convert a persistent have-not nation into a developer and even a supplier of advanced weapons on its own account, master of its own arsenal. Iraq is the latest, vivid example; consider only its modern howitzers and upgraded Scuds. But we should not forget the convincing nuclear and missile precedents of China, Israel, India, South Africa, Brazil, Argentina, Pakistan, and, for a brief moment, North Korea, a state already long active in the missile trade.

With the self-imposed exception of Brazil and Argentina, all six or seven countries, with outside help that was sometimes legal, sometimes not, endeavored to manufacture their own nuclear explosives and mostly succeeded. This clearly demonstrates that even the most esoteric and closely guarded of weapons technologies can be mastered through determined commitment, and sometimes by using the resources of personnel, of investment, of raw materials, and of political capital made available for one or another reason from overseas, sometimes unwittingly. The worldwide effort is measurable at tens of thousands of skilled person-years and totals (crudely) a billion dollars.

The partners of the lesser nuclear states are easy to name with good reliability: for China, the Soviets, who lived to repent of it; for Israel, both France and the United States; for India, Canada; for South Africa, Germany (and in the second order, Israel). Pakistan had Dutch and German aid, and perhaps Chinese as well. Only North Korea had no evident foreign associate.

Specialized technological trade, both legal and extralegal, the training of specialists overseas, and then local production, form the "supply side" of proliferation. These processes attract keen attention from earnest arms controllers and eager weapons merchants alike. But there is certainly a "demand side" to proliferation as well: the many fears and ambitions that compel less-developed nations to acquire advanced weapons, even all the way to nuclear bombs. In its effort to stem weapons proliferation, the industrialized North has scarcely addressed this demand side. Here we argue that only a sincere concern about demand promises a firm end to proliferation. Supply-side controls are mainly small steps; they may be easy to implement, although they are numerous and shift over time. The computer power at Los Alamos and Princeton that allowed the design of the earliest successful thermonuclear device was unmatched in the world of the 1950s; now MANIAC is rivaled by any $10,000 workstation. Supply-side controls are bound in the long run to fail because of leakage; good controls may slow the leaks, but they cannot stop them in our industrializing world.

Awareness must widen beyond the *symptoms* of weapons proliferation to its *causes*. It is intentions and needs, not just capabilities, that ought to become the main focus of international attention. It seems easier to control *supply*, yet it is the distant pull of *demand* that raises the tide of proliferation. Even if some prohibition measure offers the best opportunity close at hand to retard the spread of advanced weapons technologies, only serious attention to the demand side can arrest that spread in the long run.

The Causes of Demand

Weapons, the more effective the better, are perceived not only as tools for winning war but also as prized metaphors of political power and even of secure national sovereignty. The advantage at large scale may in itself suffice to hold a menacing neighbor or even an aggrieved minority in check.

Aggressive use of weapons ranges all the way from tacit intimidation to forceful seizure of such productive resources as land, oil, water, industrial capacity, and vital routes. Iraq's attempt to annex Kuwait for gold and oil, as well to end Kuwaiti oil-market maneuvers, is only the most recent example. During World War II, both Germany and Japan had hoped for such profit from aggression. Their catastrophic failure, and the global importance of those nations today, plainly based on economic and no longer on ready military strength, contain lessons that have so far not been grasped by more recent aspirants for profit and power through aggression.

Defensive needs as well do create demand for imported high-tech weapons among less-developed countries. Protection from iron-fisted pressure or even forced entry on the part of big First World forces, defense through the achievement of military symmetry with some potential adversary, are tasks to which powerful weapons can be put to hopeful use. Possession of advanced weapons, even if imported, often also confers upon a developing nation an aura of technological sophistication and status and on occasion can even induce solid technological progress. As much status symbols as instruments of combat, high-tech weapons are widely coveted: supersonic

jets, antiair missiles, airborne command and control systems, orbital surveillance, and at the limit nuclear weapons and other weapons systems
capable of mass destruction or battlefield superiority. The demand is real
and often earnest. It is, on occasion, also encouraged by First World
weapons producers; the arms race between Turkey and Greece is a vivid
example.

Misreading recent history has sustained this demand for weapons in the
Second and Third worlds. For thousands of years, the history of war has
sent a single message: weapons and their users confer political status and
power; the more plentiful and effective, the more prestige they bestow. For
many governments of the South, such axioms confirm their perception that
the surest way to resolve conflict in one's favor is by fighting and winning,
an approach that requires military superiority, in turn best assured by the
acquisition and ready use of ever more advanced armaments.

What much of the developing world has missed is the most recent double
lesson. On the one hand, notice the economic collapse of the Soviet Union
under the burden of a militarized economy, and the echoing industrial
decline of the United States during its long excessive emphasis on armaments; on the other, witness the ascending political power of Germany and
Japan, the fruit of economic strength rather than of military might. Real
power no longer comes, if it ever did, mainly from the barrels of guns, but
also from industrial success and the fiscal strength of central banks. The
futility of proliferating practices in reaching for power and gain is best
illustrated in the case of Iraq: it succeeded brilliantly in transplanting to
the banks of the Euphrates sophisticated weapons technologies and communications systems, yet its recidivist policy in Kuwait failed as soon as
Russia withheld its support.

Nevertheless, although in a world increasingly dominated by economic
considerations, weapons, even sophisticated ones, promise diminishing
returns on the battlefield, they increasingly constitute the currency with
which weak states purchase the political and diplomatic goodwill of powerful states. Saudi Arabia and the United Arab Emirates are the most recent
and vivid examples of this new proliferation dynamic. The proliferators
here are the industrial states and not the buyers of the hardware. The
demand is induced by the suppliers. Proliferation becomes the mechanism
by which the treasure of weaker or foolish nations is transferred to the

weapons industries of the North rather than being invested locally. That is the road to continuing asymmetries between North and South that in turn cause the instability and long-term conditions for conflict and war. The gains for the North are short term and temporary.

Why Stop Nuclear Proliferation?

A widely shared conviction in the industrialized North is that, unlike the case of conventional armaments, proliferation of *nuclear weapons* beyond the initial "nuclear five" must be stopped. While nuclear combat between two nuclear states will always tend toward a symmetrical negative-sum final state of devastated losers and no winner, there remain instances of asymmetrical possession in which the use of nuclear explosives is still thinkable. The easiest to grasp is the "free ride" realized in 1945 by the United States: only one of the adversaries possessed such weapons.

Fear of nuclear asymmetry, especially with respect to a particular rival, has been the prime motive of nuclear proliferation: Stalin had cause to fear the American nuclear monopoly, and the Chinese the Soviet bomb. Israel saw itself greatly outnumbered. India found nuclear asymmetry with China intolerable, and Pakistan followed the well-trodden path along with India. Until 1998 a few unassembled weapons were held on either side in a state of plausible stability with which we and they all contrived to live. But in May of that year India tested five nuclear devices of relatively low yield, suggesting they have a better store of workable models. Pakistan predictably followed suit later in the month with test explosions of its own.

Given the sharp, binary asymmetry between nuclear haves and have-nots, nuclear weapons can be, and certainly have been, instruments of tacit coercion. The same efforts at nuclear nonproliferation that nuclear powers view as prudent steps to maintain their special status are viewed by many have-nots as instances of "nuclear imperialism." Such diametrically opposed interests cannot be balanced forever by simple supply-side attempts that would deny access to specific nuclear technology in a world where advanced technology grows steadily more available. Only a wider sharing of security and decision making, one that addresses the demand side of nuclear proliferation, will attract the have-nots to permanent nuclear abstinence.

The argument for wider possession of nuclear weapons is not totally devoid of merit: nuclear proliferation would promote a symmetry of capabilities that would restrict the opportunity of nuclear powers to intimidate the have-nots. But it is a perilous symmetry that moves the community of nations away from the safety of nuclear abolition. Proliferation will make abolition much harder. It would also generate regional strategic, and tactical, instabilities and perpetuate a state of conflict and tension among neighboring nations that will distract them from the problems spawned by the demographic transition and the looming environmental degradation. Our concern is less with the increased probability of nuclear war caused by proliferation than with the indirect effects of an unyielding nuclear confrontation among neighboring states.

Why Stop Conventional Proliferation?

Beyond fear of nuclear arms, many in the North oppose the unchecked proliferation of *advanced conventional weapons* to the developing South for two mutually reinforcing concerns. First, steep gradients between North and South in standard of living, rate of development, sense of security, and even population density now form a fault line that divides the two worlds. The concern in the North is that sales of sophisticated conventional weapons to less-developed countries encourage militarism and dictatorships, squander scarce foreign currency, perpetuate underdevelopment, and indurate the prosperity gradient, the root cause of political and military tensions between North and South. The warning is clear: spreading ever more advanced conventional weapons systems to developing nations injures the long-term security of that sixth of the world's population that constitute the advanced industrialized North.

The second concern is the diminishing return from the North's efforts to improve its weapons, revealing the limitations of any technology. In the past the North could always count on possessing weapons that stood one generation ahead of its exports to less-developed nations, but this controlling superiority of modernization and efficacy is now fast fading. Many weapons have all but reached a qualitative asymptote: even marginal improvements in their performance can now be achieved only at prohibitive cost. When it exports advanced weapons, the North cannot any longer confidently count on a successor generation of more sophisticated systems that can assure its traditional technological superiority over less-developed nations. Many important weapons systems may offer no visible and affordable technological horizon with decisively superior performance. Can the United States envision a more formidable a tank than the MIA3 Abrams? Withholding the supply of ammunition and spare parts in times of hostilities may render even the most sophisticated weapon exports unusable, but the Reagan administration's sale of spare parts and ammunition to embargoed Iran through Israel shows that supply prohibitions are not airtight even when only democratic governments act.

Weapons proliferation also runs contrary to more immediate U.S. foreign policy concerns: the extension of human rights, the promotion and protection of democracy, the achievement of predictable stability worldwide. In many developing nations, proliferation inflates arsenals that help sustain military dictatorships or encourage aggression for economic gain. This is perhaps the most pernicious effect of weapons proliferation: it encourages the conviction among nations, often the ones least able to afford it, that the best way to resolve conflict is to "fight it out." The instability and endemic wars that result are contrary to what the American public has long seen as the deep interest of the United States, and directly contradicts the purpose and mission of the United Nations.

In as many as two dozen developing countries the adverse effects of disproportionate military expenditures on their economic development are visible for all to see. Weapons purchases siphon scarce foreign currency from national treasuries that otherwise could be used to promote prosperity or meliorate environmental performance. So far at least the well-being of the North faces its gravest threat not from poor-world armies equipped with superior weapons but from waves of desperate migrants crossing the Mediterranean, the Rio Grande, or the Oder, even the barrier beaches of Long Island. Such threats do not respond directly to supply-side cutoffs of weapons, but they can be lessened by honest attention and systematic assistance to address the root causes of the demand for advanced weapons by less-developed lands. Not altruism but hard-headed logic dictates this longer-term approach, minimized or neglected up to now by complacent governments in the North.

The net effect of the continuing spread of sophisticated conventional weapons is the transfer of resources from developing and underdeveloped nations to the weapons industries of the North, a new facet of the enduring practices that have deepened the asymmetry in standards of living between North and South. Arms sales, then, are exactly opposite to our prescription for a stable and peaceful world. The spread of sophisticated conventional weapons is spherically injurious to the hopes for orderly progress toward a less fractious world by the middle of the next century.

Supply-Side Measures Fade

So far efforts to stanch the proliferation of advanced weapons, especially nuclear arms, have focused mainly on the control of their supply. But it is inherent even in the best organized barriers to arms technology transfers, always founded on myriad technical details, that over the years they spring leaks. In the long run supply-side nuclear nonproliferation efforts led by nuclear states will fail by leakage, just as they did in China and South Africa, Pakistan and India, and began to do in Iraq. A developing nation with maturing industrial infrastructure can accelerate its mastery of scientific and technological nuclear know-how by determined and astute investment of resources. Supply-side efforts are a necessity; they can certainly retard the emergence of a deliverable nuclear weapon there, but can never prevent it indefinitely.

Demand-side efforts are more promising in the long run. Even nations that cannot be forced away from them can be *convinced* not to acquire nuclear weapons, as Brazil and Argentina have recently demonstrated. South Africa took the next step and destroyed its few assembled nuclear weapons. Denuclearization occurred where supply-side efforts had failed to attain it.

Three sets of circumstances will increasingly limit the ability of supply-side measures to arrest the migration of modern *conventional* armaments from North to South. First is the overabundance of weapons and weapons manufacturing capacity in the North, now that the Cold War has ended. Excess weapons manufacturing capacity in France, England, Germany, Italy, and the United States, among others, has intensified efforts to sell weapons to developing nations. The recently independent but nearly destitute republics of the former Soviet Union, laden with mighty weapons and idle capacity for their production, could also be ready providers. China continues large arms sales, evenhandedly in some cases to both sides of a war, and such small active suppliers as the Czech Republic, Israel, South Africa, and Brazil, are always ready to exploit any sales reluctance among the major weapons powers. As long as demand for high-tech weapons persists, commerce is apt to respond.

A second factor that obviates supply-side nonproliferation efforts is the rising sophistication of *civilian* technology. In areas of intense commercial competition—logic and memory chips, software, guidance and naviga-tion, telecommunications—civilian products rival or outpace military R& D in capabilities and performance. Many industrialized countries—Ger-many, Japan, Holland, France, and Italy, for example—where military R&D has always totaled a small fraction of the national R&D effort—make extensive use of civilian subcomponents in critical areas of weapons systems such as aircraft and missile guidance, control computers, and elec-tro-optical sensors.

In the United States, a long-familiar trend has reversed during the past decade: instead of civilian products "spinning off" from military research, military hardware is now increasingly assembled from subsystems and components invented and developed in the civilian sector. "Dual-use" products cannot very well be kept from prospective weapons builders else-where in the world by supply-side antiproliferation efforts.

A third effect exacerbates this trend. The automobile and robotics indus-tries, among others, are now incorporating into civilian products (smart highways, computer-controlled automotive engines, autonomous flexible manufacturing robots, geographic positioning systems) many components comparable in technological sophistication to those now employed on advanced military aircraft, or even on missiles. These technologies too will spread. Multinational industrial firms, coproduction agreements, and international consortia for research and development all facilitate the rapid diffusion of "dual-use" technologies more or less equally suitable for civil-ian or military applications.

Under all these circumstances, supply-side nonproliferation seems like putting off to sea in a sieve. Survival is temporary. There is no longer a decisive way to prohibit by denial and control the indigenous development of advanced weapons outside the North. It will be increasingly difficult in the long run, probably even futile, to attempt to stem that proliferation by supply-side measures alone. Determined embargoes and solemnly proclaimed agreements among producer nations that proscribe the export of sensitive military technologies and components will less and less suffice. Control of weapons proliferation by constraints on technology export, even in the distasteful area of denial of training and publication in basic technology, will in the end spring leaks manifestly hard to plug, especially since nonproliferation is a policy not uniformly subscribed to in the industrial North.

The Osirak Route

Concern about the inefficacy of supply-side nonproliferation has spawned a new policy in the United States—that of counterproliferation. In case supply-side measures fail to prevent the emergence of nuclear weapons in new lands controlled by undesirable regimes, the American military wants to be prepared to destroy them and the facilities for their development, production, and storage. U.S. forces should be able to "seize, disable, or destroy" such weapons of mass destruction, even at the mere "request of a threatened ally."

To be able to conduct such missions, the U.S. weapons laboratories proposed the development of earth-penetrating mini-nukes, anticipating that the Osirak experience, in which Israel attacked an above-ground Iraqi reactor in 1980, would not be duplicated, since clandestine reactors would go underground. The task of developing these new weapons, the laboratories asserted, would require testing them—reason for the United States not to agree to a ban on underground nuclear testing. Counterproliferation is also invoked to justify both theater and nationwide defenses against ballistic missiles.

The concept of counterproliferation is based on the dubious assumption that deterrence will not work in the case of new holders of nuclear fire. There is no historical or practical basis for such a view. Would Iran accept the loss of its sacred city of Qom in order to destroy Tel Aviv? Would the present or a future Saddam Hussein sacrifice Baghdad so that he can use nuclear weapons in the battlefield?

The lessons of the debate over antiballistic missile systems seem to have been lost on the advocates of counterproliferation. If ballistic missiles have nuclear warheads, defenses against them are futile because even if only a few incoming missiles escape destruction, they will annihilate their targets. If they carry conventional high explosives, they are not militarily significant because ballistic missiles are intrinsically inaccurate and so not worth defending against; they are merely instruments of terror, as were the Nazi V2 and the Scuds of the Middle East.

Preparing for Osirak-type preemptive strikes against nuclear weapons-making facilities is roundly unsound, either because such facilities reside deep underground and cannot be dug up with conventional explosives, or because they are on the surface and their destruction will release unknowable amounts of radioactivity into the environment. Even though exposed to such attack, the North Korean nuclear installations are immune because their destruction would shower radioactivity on Japan, China, or far-eastern Russia at the very least.

Counterproliferation—a transparent military-industrial pretense to continue cherished projects such as new nuclear warheads and various "sons of Star Wars" (the latter the ballistic-missile defense system initiated by the Reagan administration)—tends to produce the opposite result from its stated goal. And continuation of U.S. nuclear testing and anticipation of the eventual failure of the Non-Proliferation Treaty (NPT) may become a self-fulfilling prophecy. As nonholders of nuclear weapons perceive the United States adding to its nuclear arsenal, and expending unjustified sums on nuclear defenses, they will be more tempted to believe that nuclear weapons are worth acquiring.

Demand-Side Nonproliferation Measures for Conventional Weapons

The necessity for sincere demand-side nonproliferation measures emerges from the realization that supply-side efforts did not, cannot, and will not by themselves stem proliferation. The demand-side approach begins with serious, sincere attention to the needs and motives that impel governments to seek advanced weapons, even the means of mass destruction. The approach will require imposing heavy yet still self-serving political and economic burdens on the nations of the North. But those burdens will be lightly borne compared with the cost of preparing once again for nuclear war, for chronic instability, or for ceaseless waves of poor migrants at the shores and runways of the prosperous North.

Both positive and negative measures, the proverbial carrot and stick, are necessary to discourage demand for advanced weapons inspired by the aggressive motive of war for profit and power. Negative measures extend to the threat or use of international forces in collective action to deny aggressors any prospect of gain. Over time the realization that acquiring weapons will not result in gain will lessen demand.

But a more positive long-run approach is the systematic investment of Northern resources in the development of Southern nations, so that gains can be anticipated and realized without war weapons and war. For example, the World Bank and the International Monetary Fund could condition extension of credit to developing nations on their willingness to avoid spending foreign currency on acquiring weapons. Such a model antiproliferation measure would allow governments of recipient nations to curb their demand for advanced weapons or prepare to lose their access to international credit. If adopted as well by private lending institutions of the North, such a policy would slowly extinguish the demand for sophisticated weapons by many militarist regimes and dictatorships around the world. The approach would mainly influence smaller nations that lack the capacity for fully indigenous weapons production, but in those cases it could become decisive.

The demand for weapons to protect against aggression, or to rectify a threatening military asymmetry with an expansionist neighbor, can be addressed by offering positive guarantees of prompt intervention by a permanent international armed force. Collective opposition to Iraq's invasion of Kuwait, even though assembled on an ad hoc basis, provides something of a model. Such a force can one day be institutionalized to avoid the implications of single-state control. The conditions and procedures for committing this common security force to the defense of threatened nations will have to be clearly articulated from the start and then evolve in practice. The goal should surely be not only to counter aggression, but also to deter it before it occurs. We take up this important topic in the next chapter.

The widest possible participation among nations will be essential. An international force with responsibility for deterring or opposing aggression will require advanced and intricate weapons systems and the organizations to deploy them, including transport, command, control, communications, reconnaissance, and intelligence, as well as special air and naval forces usually held by the militarily prepared nations of the North. All governments would have to designate, equip, support, train, and honor (yes, and eventually pension!) a portion of their armed forces to stand as part of the Common Security force, although nations of the South could supply many of the ground troops. Combined training also needs to be provided. The credibility and reliability of international Collective Security can grow only gradually. Governments will not forego either their reliance on national armies or their demand for modern weapons overnight. Confidence will build slowly with repeated successes of collective opposition to aggression, but it will tend to flag over any single hesitation.

Such an approach will never be a panacea for all armed turbulence. Clear-cut cases of aggression can be expected to trigger quick reflexive response from a standing international force even when vital interests of major nations are not involved. But internal chronic strife, with deep-seated emotional roots, as in Lebanon in the 1980s or Bosnia at the present, will probably remain outside the perimeter of such timely involvement for a long time.

Coherent long-term development assistance from the North to Second and Third World nations is also an important facet of dampening weapons proliferation. Growing economies in the South would create markets for the industrial products and services of the North, and efforts in the South to improve environmental performance would also benefit the North.

Successful demand-side antiproliferation measures will need consistent and impartial attention over an extended period of time, but demand for new weapons will eventually wither. By comparison supply-side efforts must be maintained indefinitely, even when successful, to counter continual, unattended demand. The advantage of demand-side efforts is clear.

Demand-Side Nonproliferation Measures for Nuclear Weapons

The demand for nuclear weapons that arises from the fear of nuclear asymmetry with a neighbor can also be attenuated with positive guarantees. In chapter 5 we consider the eventual establishment of a temporary multinational nuclear deterrent force consisting of four nuclear ballistic-missile submarines on loan from the United States, Russia, France, the United Kingdom, and China.

Worse-case scenarios that delimit the potential application of so terrifying a force are easy to construct. What if Israel, threatened with extinction by a pan-Arab attack, used nuclear weapons on the battlefield—would the international force nuke Tel Aviv? This false dilemma would not occur because an international community well prepared to meet aggression anywhere could dissuade Israel from using nuclear weapons. Participants in a regime of Common Security would be likely to use nuclear weapons only against nuclear users.

A more difficult scenario still invokes a truly reckless government. What if some state dropped a nuclear weapon in the Saudi desert as extortionary warning, threatening an attack on Riyadh, and then actually destroyed the city upon Saudi refusal to comply with their demands? Would the international nuclear force obliterate the responsible capital, especially if that rogue government threatened to destroy an innocent third party, say Alexandria, in retaliation? In such a scenario the international nuclear force would assure the reckless leadership that such a course would result only in physical occupation (a task that the international force could facilitate by battlefield use of nuclear weapons), punishment and replacement of the leadership, and long-term reparations to injured parties.

An unusual degree of cooperation among nuclear club members will surely be necessary: ceding exclusive possession of strong nuclear forces will require considerable political courage. But the price is small compared with the cost of preparing to avoid nuclear destruction of their own cities, as Soviet citizens can testify. Utopian though it may appear so soon after the Cold War, a multinational nuclear force, firmly controlled by a broadened U.N. Security Council that includes Germany, Japan, and, say, Brazil or a democratic Nigeria as permanent members, could dampen the demand and so the spread of nuclear weapons worldwide.

The formation of an international nuclear force as the intermediate step on the road toward complete elimination of nuclear arsenals would be in the enlightened self-interest of the nuclear club of five. Such a force would not constitute an absolute guarantee against all conceivable nuclear acts of aggression. But by providing a potential nuclear counter to any nuclear aggressor threatening a nonnuclear nation, it would establish the self-same symmetry that prevented nuclear nations from using nuclear weapons against each other during the long Cold War.

The design of such a structure would require thought. There would be a particular need for sure measures for identifying the origin of nuclear weapons, both technical schemes and penalties that extend culpability to careless and errant states. The formation of such a multinational nuclear force would also be a useful stopgap measure that could address the security needs of a number of potential proliferators, until the symmetry of uniform nonpossession of nuclear weapons can be reached. A multinational nuclear force that can be seen as the intimidating instrument of the existing club of the nuclear five cannot maintain the nuclear peace indefinitely. It will be acceptable *only* as an intermediate step to global nuclear abstinence.

A much more benign cause for nuclear arming is more probable in the future than the grim prospects we have just considered. We must credit the North Koreans and the South Africans for its invention. At a time of economic distress and diplomatic isolation brought about in both cases by international ostracism, North Korea appears to have attempted, and South Africa completed, the development of nuclear weapons. It seems to us that in both cases the purpose was to induce the intervention of the United States, and by extension, the rest of the industrialized North. South Africa could not plan military use of nuclear explosives to resolve its racial difficulties. But revealing its ownership of nuclear bombs in the midst of a threatening civil war between blacks and whites there might have brought a U.S. military presence. This would have constituted much more effective security than the possession of half a dozen nuclear weapons.

The case of North Korea is both prototypical and paradigmatic. Isolated diplomatically and economically, bereft of external aid after the collapse of the Soviet Union, that country failed to attract the attention of the world except when it allowed its incipient nuclear facilities to be seen in a bomb-making mode. By refusing their inspection the North Koreans were able to maintain the nuclear charade and succeed! The United States promised, quite wisely, several billion dollars in aid and diplomatic recognition.

This novel use of nuclear technology, even if make-believe, will find emulators in the future among nations of the developing and underdeveloped worlds as they struggle with the effects of demographic transition. If the North ignores, even benignly, their plight, the surest way to attract attention and aid would be by abandoning the Non-Proliferation Treaty and initiating "visibly secret" nuclear bomb activities. Their demand for nuclear weapons will be, ab initio at least, nonmilitary; but persistent indifference of the industrial North may eventually change that. The nuclear club of five would have to respond to this demand not for power but for economic and technological aid that would ease the stresses of the demographic transition. Optimally, as we suggest in later chapters, attention to the developing and underdeveloped world should be planned, systematic, and persistent, rather than in reaction to nuclear fears.

Most demand-side antiproliferation measures will require lengthy preparations, leading to unusual cooperation among the wealthy and powerful nations of the North. To impede proliferation supply-side efforts will have to continue and expand, though we remain fully aware that export controls and technology embargoes have useful but well-circumscribed capabilities. Those measures can slow the flow of sophisticated systems and weapons of mass destruction, but only demand-side efforts can finally dry it up.

Our Recommendations

The reduction of militarization worldwide is a constant goal. Eventual rectification of the asymmetry of five nuclear states in an otherwise nonnuclear world is ahead. Smoothing the sharp asymmetries in standard of living and rate of development between the advanced industrialized North and the second- and third-tier nations in the South can be a first step. Measures that would reduce the economic disparities between China and Japan, Mexico and the United States, or Poland and Germany are examples. Attention to the steep gradients in the economic landscape is part and parcel of the demand-side nonproliferation effort. Mutual fear must be replaced by mutual aid in a world tending over many decades toward safety and well-being for all. Common Security can oppose decisively those countries that dissent aggressively from this vision for any reason and attempt instead to gain needed change by large-scale military violence.

The resources in treasure and talent now devoted to supporting the military worldwide are immense by any standard—now three-quarters of a trillion dollars per year. A most reassuring feature of the present world economy is that only a fraction of that sum, if devoted to development, could achieve in time peacefully what weapons can never do: profoundly improve the standard of living and security for all nations, producing a world with not just winners over losers but one where everyone begins to win. Surely the North will have to pay in reduced consumption for a great gain in stability and peace. The South can pay in patience for the end of inequality and injustice, to gain reasoned hope and freedom from the threat of overwhelming conflict. If North-South asymmetries in opportunity and in security both moderate, conflict and fear will tend to diminish, the demand for weapons will gradually fade, and within a few decades weapons proliferation may become a thing of the past. Nuclear weapons will decline in number and in readiness; in the end they will fall asleep, even as the tritium decays, over the next handful of decades. This is a reachable outcome, not a utopian proposal. It requires a fundamental change of attitudes and practices by both North and South. This is exactly what we propose.

The United States can initiate, encourage, and support an effective demand-side nonproliferation policy to parallel its current attention to the supply side. Eleven steps, in incremental order of difficulty, some familiar and immediate, some novel and long-lasting, sketch a beginning toward that hopeful future.

• Stop developing, testing, and producing any new nuclear weapons immediately and permanently.

• Declare a policy of no first use of nuclear weapons, contingent on an agreement among all nuclear powers to do the same.

• Initiate negotiations among the members of the nuclear club aiming at the eventual monitored, operational elimination of all nuclear weapons, to be held for a long time only in abeyance, as deterrents to first use. Such talks might be called at the initiative of the new nuclear powers in the Indian subcontinent, where such a status seems incipient. There it ought first to become declaratory and thereafter both binding and monitored.

• Sponsor and support the admission of Germany and Japan, along with a few large nations from unrepresented continents, as new permanent members of the U.N. Security Council, with veto power, to give the council more credibility.

• Strengthen supply-side nonproliferation measures by agreeing to end most arms sales, with more rigorous policing of secondhand transfers and judicious physical control of "dual-use" technologies when and where possible.

• Focus conventional-weapons R&D on improving the reliability, immunity to countermeasures, and cost of existing major weapons systems. Refrain from developing major new weapons, such as combat aircraft or tank-killer helicopters, especially those with long-range capability.

• Organize a global banking and credit embargo against extravagant purchasers of weapons.

• Extend large-scale civilian aid to developing and underdeveloped countries, and phase out all military financial aid and loans worldwide.

• Assist the United Nations in developing a many-sided set of long-term peaceful measures for peacemaking and early resolution of specific conflicts. These can include published studies of their origin and course; joint education and negotiations, binding and nonbinding, among representatives of parties in conflict; publicly broadcast communications; and provision for prosecuting crimes against the peace.

• Initiate negotiations under U.N. sponsorship to raise a permanent, international common security force, perhaps divided into regional commands, and designate U.S. units—Marines, Air Force, Navy, and space assets—to be part of this force, with appropriate training, equipment, recognition, and support.

• Initiate consultations among the United States, United Kingdom, Russia, France, and China on forming an international nuclear deterrent force of ballistic missile submarines as a final resort, to be controlled by an expanded U.N. Security Council. This implies a kind of "death penalty" upon other peoples and nations, and would thus rightly be unacceptable to many. But the issue needs to be faced. We return to this in more detail in the next chapter.

5

Common Security

In the second half of this century the human enterprise has afforded us time and again the occasion to recognize the unitary character of human existence on this Earth—above all those pictures sent by the American astronauts of a blue Earth rising over a drab moonscape. Then came the ubiquitous dangers of a deteriorating environment that recognize no national frontiers. Still earlier had come the most vivid reminder by far of our common fate, the realization of the inexorably shared disaster of a large-scale nuclear war.

Such is the nature of nuclear weapons that any unilateral choices and measures undertaken by any nation, no matter how earnest and costly, cannot end or much reduce its vulnerability to the symmetric nuclear destruction of both combatants in a nuclear war. Beginning in the nuclear era the security that up to then was unilaterally sought through effort to emerge as the winner in a zero-sum war was reduced to a symmetric impasse: either both adversaries were secure or neither was. Traditional efforts to provide national security by the competitive unilateral accumulation of military forces could not relieve the frightful symmetry. The realization of indivisible common security has dawned. Persistent exertions to gain meaningful military superiority during the Cold War spawned an unprecedented gigantism of military means yet did not achieve their goal. The military establishments on either side of the East-West ideological divide grew grotesquely large, and preparations for a war between the two blocs that was futile a priori became astronomically costly. Pervasive and determined efforts on both sides distorted the economies and societies of a large part of the industrialized North. Yet security remained attainable only when shared.

The futile exertions to achieve unilateral security instead inflated insecurity and created a scale for judging the adequacy of military preparedness for national security that was grossly out of proportion by any peacetime standards. The nuclear era taught us that achieving national security—preserving the integrity, sovereignty, and political freedom of a nation, and the physical and psychological security of its citizens—does not require a zero-sum approach to international relations. It does not have to be achieved at the expense of the security of another nation. Common Security is not only possible but in fact is the only realistic doctrine that can replace deterrence and not risk Armageddon by zeal or miscalculation.

Peace Preserved by Joint War

It is firmly to Mikhail Gorbachev's credit that he first acted on the recognition of the futility of military competition between East and West and so initiated an end to the high arms race. The collapse of the command economies shortly thereafter transformed the binary standoff of the past half-century into a fluid, nearly unitary community of nations. Since then, for the first time in recorded history, the major powerful nations of the world have been in loose resonance, still pursuing their self-interests but collectively, sharing common decisions that they impose and try to maintain cooperatively. The Northern industrialized states are no longer in two camps, but are beginning to form a community with intertwined interests to curb their competition. Economically emerging, politically aloof China, still marked by deep regional cleavages, appears more eager to compete than to confront. We will say much more about this most populous of countries.

With the East-West fault line smoothed, attention among the developed nations is now focusing on the much deeper divide that parts North from South, rich from poor. There the asymmetry is more striking, not only in standard of living, security, and hope, but in political and military influence as well. As silicon rivals copper and graphite fibers replace steel, industrial production "dematerializes," with the result that there is less and less besides coffee, oil, narcotics, and cheap but careful assembly labor that the South can offer to or withhold from the North. (This change is still in progress and is by no means complete.) Saddam Hussein's bold annexation of Kuwait, and the threat of subsequent subordination of Saudi Arabian resources, can be seen as an attempt to control enough of the oil supply of the North to become a sizable Southern power, able to counterbalance the overwhelming dominance of the industrial states. But that was so contrary to the common interest of the North *and* of Iraq's neighbors that it was promptly defeated under U.S. lead but aided and mostly paid for by common effort.

The utter defeat of Iraq confirmed the continuing weakness of the South, and signaled the collective determination of the industrialized nations to remain in control. It also defined de facto the scale and mode of future wars: since the probability of real war among the developed nations appears receding to the vanishing point, future Common Security military operations will address only one or a few of the nations of the South or the fragments of once-large multinational states. In either case the size of the military forces and the level of their preparation can for decades to come amount only to a small fraction of the gigantic military establishments of the Cold War superpowers. Aggressive behavior by any of the larger developing nations will have mainly to be countered, ab initio at least, not by military effort—which remains too costly for any but the most extreme cases—but by civilian intervention, from mediation to embargoes to boycotts, and on to blockades and arrest and trial of individual war criminals.

Desert Storm, the hundred-hour ground operation that defeated Iraq, was both a paradigmatic and a calibrating instance of a brief Common Security regime. (The war in Korea was fought from 1950 to 1953 in the name of the United Nations, but in fact was overtly a campaign of the Cold War between East and West.) The Gulf War of 1991 showed that the foundation of Common Security can be a common interest, implying that collective action against transborder aggression is likely whenever the common interests of the major powers coincide and are clearly threatened.

But a Common Security regime based on this principle would soon lead to counterproductive results: the South, both the developing and the less-developed regions, would remain politically and militarily disproportionately weak. The history of multinational ad hoc interventions provides ample evidence: Korea, Iraq, Somalia, Rwanda, and Bosnia are all examples of interventions hastily organized either to oppose transborder aggression injurious to industrialized states, or to pacify the humanitarian instincts of TV viewers. Those interventions were instigated and led by the United States without due preparation or a priori established rules of engagement.

Neither Bosnia nor Somalia were cases of transborder aggression but rather instances of what we may without irony call a modern form of tribal war. They arose from a deep substratum of history, adroitly newly uncovered for political effect. They might not have qualified as occasions for peer-approved military intervention by the developed world, since they did not threaten its vital economic or strategic interests. Nor did they constitute intolerable cases of aggression that, if left unanswered, would induce instability and disorder and erode the rule of law among nations.

In the particular case of Bosnia, the United States finally intervened. One motive was surely to balance the strong anti-Islamic impression that the easy U.S. rollback of Iraq created among some oil-holding Muslim states. No principle of Common Security but rather diplomatic expediency has often been at work so far in collective intervention; Iraq may have marked a turning point.

Even though individual developed nations have displayed some willingness to oppose aggression and so quench war among Southern states, and even though the forces necessary to do so would often be quite modest, the developed lands have been loathe recently to involve themselves in such confrontations. They might well be perceived, both by many of their own citizens and by the world community, as forceful self-serving interventions characteristic of earlier colonialist days. While aggression cannot be allowed to succeed because it creates a precedent that would encourage international chaos, unilateral opposition to it by one nation of the North would prove so difficult to support politically that aggression might go unopposed unless worthy multinational action were organized. As a result, common opposition to transborder aggression is not merely the sufficient means, but rather the necessary means to safeguard peace through collective military intervention. The way common opposition has been organized until now offers no added security to the nations outside the industrialized North. Consequently it does not yet fully serve the purpose of Common Security: to reduce national armed forces worldwide.

Half a century after they were enunciated, the ideals of the U.N. charter are slowly becoming feasible, as practical considerations encourage powerful nations to adopt a proper Common Security doctrine. Such a doctrine permits the sharing of risks, of preparations for war, and of their costs, including the risks of combat casualties. The doctrine reduces sharply the risk of bilateral nationalistic confrontations and can give individual states the option to remain uninvolved in any given military operation, only fractionally reducing the ability of the rest to counter aggression through U.N. collective action.

Fundamental differences exist between the ad hoc, unprepared, and narrowly based common actions against aggression the world has so far seen, and the regime of Common Security we put forth here as the necessary intermediate state between present and future security arrangements. In fact, we believe that the hesitance and mistrust many governments display toward joined military interventions derives precisely from these differences. Except in the case of Bosnia, intervention has occurred in the South. Yet the input of Southern states was mostly pro forma. No institutionalized procedure exists for such participation outside the United Nations. Neither are there clear-cut rules of engagement of a Common Security force that would protect the sovereignty of individual states. Under those circumstances it is not surprising that the very concept of Common Security as perceived by many does not attract participation.

Yet the Common Security doctrine has emerged because of the current state of the species. Increasingly international problems are not bilateral ones that could be addressed by the standard mechanism of diplomacy or war, but operate on a much larger scale. They require states to come together to deal with them, or large international organizations to cope with them. Addressing the contamination of sea and air, the AIDS pandemic, and the production and consumption of psychoactive drugs come readily to mind. The needed approaches tend more to be based on reasoned, almost technocratic considerations rather than on the emotional or ideological tendencies of individual states. No day of victory is involved in countering these problems; no one's virility is tested in arriving at practical solutions for them.

Here, and in greater detail in chapter 7, we propose an orderly regime of Common Security, with permanent, well-prepared civilian and limited military capabilities to counter well-defined cases of transborder aggression. We believe that common interests tend to overshadow individual nationalist impulses. Military action when necessary will become more nearly dispassionate, more like policing. Invocations of country, the insulted flag, the honor of the ancestors, and other emotional trappings will dwindle. Combat itself will become more like surgery, mechanized, less risky, steadily demythologized, and made less murderous, more fully professional.

We do not proceed to offer detailed recipes for achieving the requisite political consensus in individual nations that can lead them to embrace Common Security practices. Domestic bureaucratic politics, important but ephemeral, easily changeable and dependent as they are on local political elites who are also changeable, form too volatile a base for our argument. We only hope to show that no fundamental objective barriers exist to such arrangements, and that the result of a properly defined and established Common Security regime can be a peaceful and stable community of nations.

Under the threat of nuclear catastrophe nations acted in the Gulf with reason, put aside the zero-sum approach to security, and embraced shared security. We are witnessing a similar trend in most countries' approach to conflict: an understandable aversion to combat. The fatal combat in central Africa or Bosnia looms important on the spot, but those are disturbances on a deep and widening pool of world consensus against warfare.

Peace through Punitive Acts of Peace: Civilian Intervention

The conjunction of large nations in the emerging unitary world makes practical both civilian—nonviolent but both coercive and conciliatory—and military interventions for maintaining peace: the imposition of a whole spectrum of international sanctions on a judged aggressor. Denying or restricting trade, aid, international credit, and key services, like telecommunications and transportation, are serious interventions; specific and varied embargoes and blockades can have powerful impact. No nation, large or small, can lead an insular existence and still maintain its share of a modern efficient and productive economy. Only large industrialized nations could perhaps reach even approximate self-sufficiency, and then only at great cost in a sharply reduced standard of living for their populations.

Canceling the results of aggression may be achievable only by military or civilian coercion, but preventing the aggression can be achieved not only by punitive means or by deterrence but by affirmative action as well, both military and civilian. Preventive measures include "positive guarantees" of collective military intervention, economic and development aid, even judicial and educational facilities that promote early negotiation of conflicts. A properly organized and functioning Common Security regime, for example, could have heeded the numerous signals of impending hostilities that were emanating from Yugoslavia beginning in 1987. Mediation, aid, guarantees of trade and inclusion—all could have helped avoid the spallation of at least Bosnia and Macedonia, even Croatia, off Yugoslavia. Together with the military and civilian "sticks" the major powers have traditionally used to maintain the peace is the imaginative and well-supported use of "carrots" toward the same end; the fruits of persuasion may well prove more lasting than the results of intimidation. Positive guarantees of outside military support in case of aggression by a neighbor can also deter the neighbor and permit the recipient nation to relax its military readiness and reduce its defense expenditures, since it will not face aggression without effective allies.

Collective military action against Iraq was an exception. It was a clear example of the impressive manner in which the doctrine of Common Security can be used to reverse change achieved by armed violence. It was not only direct punishment of aggression but also a warning to potential future aggressors that sudden violent change of borders will not be tolerated by the international community, even though in that case its roots and its power—drawn from the huge Cold War inventory—were wholly in the service of America and her close allies. Its lesson is all the same a powerful deterrent, though the way it was organized filled many nations with misgivings.

Heavy punitive military action against an aggressor is not the only path to peace. The civilian complement to "Desert Storm" is the ongoing civilian intervention against Iraq that includes the trade embargo. Embargoes have yielded misted results when used for other purposes—for example, against nations that conspicuously violated human rights, like Rhodesia and apartheid South Africa, or perpetrated grossly illegal actions against explicit agreements, such as the Turkish occupation of northern Cyprus, or more recently the Haitian military's refusal to allow President Aristide to resume office. Embargoes are slow to take hold and often affect the poor first and most painfully, but they are a punishment that eschews armed violence. Such actions are politically easier to impose at a time of consonance in the larger community of nations, and can be applied when the costs of military intervention in blood and treasure appear impractically high, as in the case of a large industrialized nation's aggression against a small one.

Aggression has been reversed or prevented by the deterring effect of threatened collective military or civilian punishment against an aggressor. But Common Security can be pursued through rewards as well. Economic aid, preferential trade treatment, easy access to inexpensive capital, or even outright grants—all made in some way conditional upon peaceful behavior and abstinence from war preparations, may be more persuasive modulators of national behavior than threats of punishment, or even actual punitive action post facto.

None of these Common Security approaches are very practical without the unanimous consent of the major powers—rarely, perhaps, a major power might simply remain a bystander—and often only through their active cooperation. At the very least acquiescence by a clear majority of the rest of the nations is also needed. Whether organized by a half-dozen of the wealthiest and most powerful nations in some ad hoc forum or formally by the United Nations through the Security Council, no Common Security measures will succeed while some important nations dissent strongly or even oppose them or the international community demurs.

The necessary cooperation can be much encouraged by expanding participation in international decision making, and by strengthening the Security Council. The inclusion as permanent Council members of economic powers like Germany and Japan, of Brazil, of India, and perhaps of other large states, such as a democratic Nigeria or Indonesia, will soon become a necessity, as will an unambiguous listing of the occasions that would merit action. Certainly the victors of World War II cannot and should not forever maintain their special roles.

The Price of Common Security

Even though the advantages of a Common Security approach to world peace are evident, the doctrine is not without weaknesses and potential obstacles. For example, the feasibility and effectiveness of a Common Security military force depends on its permanence and size. Creating a large enough force may be politically infeasible, either because the costs could not easily be borne by the United Nations, or because individual nations will remain unwilling when asked to provide the necessary forces promptly. The U.N. operation in Bosnia failed because, among other reasons, it was so poorly prepared and supported.

Building up a central Common Security force over time seems a path that evades this contradiction. Start with a U.N. brigade of only 5,000 to 8,000 soldiers, kept ready and equipped to respond to a crisis within one or two days. Then over the space of a few years augment those troops with a much larger body of 25,000 to 40,000 men and women, also trained, and visibly available on a notice of weeks or a month. The augmenting forces could be assembled as they are now—by choosing among national forces prepared and committed to serve the United Nations on request, of course at the explicit direction of some agreed-upon political body, often the Security Council.

Certainly tough political, financial, and organizational problems are inherent in efforts to establish a ready multinational Common Security contingent. The effectiveness of that force will depend as much on its physical size and readiness for varied forms and theaters of combat as on the political credibility and reliability of its response. The adequacy and with it the waxing credibility of the Common Security regime can be established gradually, chiefly as the outcome of timely and broadly justified interventions to suppress aggression. Both attributes would be worn away by cases of premature withdrawal, military defeat, or frequent procrastination, as well as by clearly partisan decisions on whether to intervene.

To avoid such pitfalls—already visible in interventions so far—it is essential that deployment procedures, the events that trigger intervention, and the required mechanisms of consultation and decision making, though certainly not the action itself, are agreed upon ahead of time (and not merely in response to any specific provocation) by all participating nations. Such clear definition of procedures and advance provision of the complex and appropriate resources and logistics for action will minimize the probability of partisan decisions, avoid procrastination, and strengthen the credibility and deterrent value of a Common Security force of any size.

At the same time a fresh political decision probably remains essential for each significant action. The perception of inequitable use of the Common Security force, or repeated national interventions that flout or supplant the common will, are the more probable when the force is not militarily effective, or when it has much less than unanimous backing of the large powers and the nations in the region of conflict. Such circumstances will become unavoidable if most major powers do not take part in common political decisions; without that unity a Common Security force can hardly become feasible in the first place.

The most conspicuous sources of armed conflict at present are internal to a single recognized nation-state: consider Bosnia, Sudan, Cambodia, Azerbaijan, Georgia, Kazakhstan, Burundi, East Timor, Sri Lanka, and many more. These are in fact instances of domestic warfare, some of them ethnic in origin, some old, some newly triggered by other changes in sovereign rule. The role of a Common Security regime in such cases is complicated by an apparent contradiction. If its mandate is restricted to cross-border conflicts only, then the common-security approach will fail to address the most frequent cause of wars. If it is meant to arrest civil wars as well, use of military force would violate the sovereignty of nations that such a force is raised to protect in the first place. This is a dilemma the United Nations has already escaped. In cases of internal conflict the United Nations provides intermediaries and civil negotiators; once both parties to the conflict agree, it emplaces peacekeeping forces (usually smaller and less heavily armed than the forces they watch over) whose rules of engagement run only to self-defense. This traditional role of the United Nations, already established and long in practice, does not entail active support of one belligerent against the other, and often has not even constituted intervention in violation of sovereign frontiers.

The rules of engagement must be clear and scrupulously observed: non-consensual military intervention by a Common Security force will be permitted, possibly even at length become automatic, only in opposition to transborder aggression. Borders will need to be formally defined under U.N. eyes. Consensual intervention is also appropriate in all instances of peacekeeping or humanitarian relief. Nations have often been tempted to intervene in civil strife on the side of their favored combatant. Even democratic states have tended to intervene to support nondemocratic factions who might become allies—a policy that has inflamed rather than dampened civil war. In Vietnam in the 1960s and in Afghanistan in the 1980s, active intervention proved catastrophic because it was ideologically or strategically partisan. Powerful outside intervenors appeared on both sides of the initial conflicts, turning them into client wars. We can expect cases in the future—such as when the military dictatorship in Haiti held sway—where most nations might move to restore to power a democratically elected government ousted by a military junta. This is intervention into civil war, no new matter (Lafayette began it in the United States long ago). It is a touchy but probably growing policy. Explicit international political approval may become the condition for serious international support.

While nations naturally abhor contributing troops to a common intervention that will sustain casualties, they have a counterbalancing fear of facing some future aggressor alone. As the United States and the former Soviet Union can testify, even very large nations cannot painlessly maintain forever large unilateral preparations for self-defense.

Nonparticipation will hardly be tolerated in the case of civilian interventions, such as embargoes and denial of credit or travel, at least when it would obviate the effectiveness of the measures. But some political exceptions can and certainly will be made; it was not expedient to force Jordan in 1991 to forego all exchange with its supplier and customer Iraq, a powerful neighbor across a land border (the Jordanian government even offered public verbal support for Iraq's campaign). But the goods the heavy trucks bore between Iraq and Jordan were not enough to vitiate the oil and trade embargo maintained by pipeline closures and tanker blockade.

Those nations not directly affected by the economic recoil of embargoes will have to compensate, at least partially, the nations most affected by lost trade with an embargoed country. Nations will then stand more ready to join, and erosion of the sanctions will be minimized. Just as military intervention has costs, so does its civilian counterpart. Such a policy is in the common interest of all—clearly cheaper than maintaining universal readiness for war without alliances.

Both in size and in the occasions of use, a Common Security force will face strict practical limits. To begin, such a force will probably not act against veto-carrying members of the U.N. Security Council as long as the council controls the force. But other large nations with well-developed militaries will not be immune to civilian punitive intervention nor indifferent to the positive approaches—both military and civilian—of the Common Security doctrine outlined. A dozen nations now have armed forces larger than several hundred thousand troops. Even if they could thwart punitive military intervention should they attempt aggressive acts, they would indeed prove vulnerable to serious civilian interventions such as trade embargoes, maintained over the long run.

A Common Security doctrine will serve peace, but it will not automatically bring justice. It will not promote injustice if properly structured, but it will not necessarily rectify it. Within its limited domain it can fulfill its promise: more stability and international order, fewer wars and fewer deaths in war, and sharply reduced military expenditures worldwide.

But while even a reliable Common Security regime would not lift the asymmetry between powerful and smaller nations, it would offer a measure of protection to the latter unavailable otherwise. This could enable many developing and less-developed nations to cut their defense expenditures, to avail themselves of the political and diplomatic influence of the world community, but at the same time to be deterred from aggressive acts. The fact that most wars now occur in the South indicates that Common Security is perhaps a necessary precursor to more peaceful conditions conducive to development.

Demand-side efforts to prevent further proliferation of nuclear weapons and conventional armaments cannot be effective without the robust presence of a Common Security regime. Why should states renounce military preparations unless they receive positive guarantees, both military and civilian? Common Security offers the possibility of essential democratization without instability. Rational political elites bent on development will see the advantages.

Making War in the Cause of Peace: How Much Force?

We examine here in more detail what occasions would trigger a Common Security response, and what level of combat a practical Common Security force would be designed to sustain. In civilized societies, law provides for nonviolent resolution of conflict and personal safety through use of the courts and organized police forces. Ceding authority to the police and the courts in exchange for a good deal of security has replaced the violent anomie of anarchic times, when at least in principle armed individuals were responsible for their own safety: all against all. An Enlightenment philosopher, Immanuel Kant, plainly advocated an obvious extension of the role of law within societies to apply among states as well. "International conflict can be settled by negotiation and diplomacy," he argued, "and order can be maintained by an international armed force."[1] Since then this concept has been promoted repeatedly, by the League of Nations in the early 1920s, more recently in the U.N. charter of 1945. The congruence of the rule of law within and among nations suggests some immediate conclusions.

Just as police do not eliminate crime completely, so we ought not expect a Common Security regime to extirpate war and aggression. And just as police do not mediate all disputes among individuals within a society, so the role and tasks of a Common Security force are limited to preventing and opposing aggression, leaving national forces to guard the internal order of nations and specially authorized international peacekeeping forces to maintain a peace already negotiated in words between international belli-cose parties. Thus the applicability of a Common Security doctrine would be confined to: (1) preventing and opposing transborder aggression, by armed military or civilian intervention—punitive or affirmative—and (2) intervening at the request of both parties in an internal "tribal," regional, or economic war to monitor the peaceful measures already agreed upon, usually with forces armed and authorized to engage only in self-defense.

The magnitude of the military effort and the most appropriate mix of intervention mechanisms will depend on the specifics of the situation and the importance of the interests at hand. Military intervention is not now indicated in the U.N. whenever the aggressor is one of the powerful states that hold veto power in the Security Council. Nor is it likely to be chosen any time soon against such newer large and well-armed developing nations as India, Brazil, Indonesia, or the Koreas, but no one is immune.

In all cases the preferred approach is incremental. First come steps such as discussion, mediation, charges brought against individuals in an international court of jurisdiction to come, withdrawal of peripheral benefits such as international sports visits. The nations might then try a variety of specific or more general embargoes on imports and exports—perhaps sea, air, or even land blockades and the credit restrictions and asset-freezing procedures available to a cooperating international community. Suspension of essential services—air travel, post and telecommunications, frontier-crossing power lines, technical cooperation—can be a last resort. Such civilian interventions must be maintained over the long term to succeed; they can be applied with flexibility and do not require the politically difficult commitment of numerous large national troop contingents. They also avoid direct violence. The increasing degree of interdependence among nations will make such collective action more effective and therefore more promising.

It is true that sanctions usually affect the people of any nation with the least power, with the leaders who bear most responsibility for a conflict avoiding suffering. Limits lie here too, but the outcome is always open to debate.

Civilian complements military intervention in those cases in which armed opposition to aggression is impractical, and so responds to one of the most serious objections to the Common Security doctrine, that it can deal effectively only with transborder aggression between small nations. Therefore, its critics say, such a doctrine is de facto a new form of Northern interventionism among the underdeveloped nations. While some states will be powerful enough to avoid common military intervention and others will not, judicious and persistent civilian intervention can level the field and affect rich and poor nations alike. The overall approach will have to grow in public esteem to induce toleration by the powerful.

Nuclear War: Capital Punishment of Nations

No analysis of the domain of applicability of the Common Security doctrine would be complete without an examination of the very worst case, one in which a nuclear-armed state attacks a nonnuclear nation with nuclear weapons. That has happened only once. A realistic threat of retaliation—not first use—by a consortium of the established nuclear nations can deter such an attack. The community may require a choice between nuclear retaliation and a less destructive attack. Consider a multinational nuclear deterrent force, consisting of four nuclear ballistic missile submarines on loan from their current possessors, the United States, Russia, France, the United Kingdom, even China, with national crews. Under international control from its sponsors, such a force, with say two submarines on ocean patrol at all times, kept on the firm leash of shore-based "go" codes, would constitute an untargetable and assured deterrent capable of inhibiting nuclear attack by any nuclear nation against any nuclear have-not. The decision to use such a terrible tool would be shared by many; the process would be elaborate and slow. But that is how it should be. The aggressor's cities cannot run away, and unlike the little-lamented multilateral forces of Cold War vintage, the nuclear deterrent of the Common Security regime won't have to fight a nuclear war. The many warheads available could span a wide range of yields, kilotons to megatons, allowing choice of the target size from, say, a communications base up to a metropolitan center. The few nations who comprise the force will probably be exempt from its warheads, de facto if not de jure.

Actual use of this international force must certainly be kept a remote possibility, a final and terrible resort. Certainly first use of nuclear weapons will not be morally or politically open to the Common Security regime; that is the act of trust that lies here. In the nuclear shadow the punishment of nuclear aggression would start with easier steps: from economic restitution to the victim of nuclear attack by the offender to greater reparations, even to required self-destruction or expatriation of some of the attacker's national assets. In the case of an obdurate aggressor, say one that might threaten nuclear attack on some nearby hostage population, especially a nonbelligerent one, the ultimate step might be nuclear destruction of one or more cities, after a genuine warning that allows for general civilian evacuation.

By providing a potential nuclear counter to any nuclear aggressor that threatens a nonnuclear nation, such a nuclear force would establish the self-same symmetry that has completely prevented nuclear nations from using nuclear weapons against each other, or even against client states during the long Cold War, even during its hot intervals in East Asia. Many issues enter the design of such a deterrent structure. In particular there is need for sure measures of identification of the origin of nuclear weapons, both by technical schemes, and by motivating structures that extend some culpability for careless or errant transfer of nuclear weapons to nonnuclear states by present holders.

There is more than a remote analogy between nuclear-armed forces used for Common Security and the death penalty. Whereas in the latter the state assumes responsibility for irreversible punitive action against a single or a few human beings, even in the presence of doubt, here the Common Security forces would destroy uninvolved citizens to punish a tyrannical leadership. How can the international community wipe out a city and surely many citizens unable or not allowed to leave in the name of peace? So cruel an act, with its concomitant fallout, must be hedged about by many safeguards, open only in extremis. Whether it can be supported at all by a regime bent on justice and peace is arguable. The eventual moral stand of the peacemakers, as of the state's executioners, will reflect the world's perception of the justice and necessity of this most punitive of actions.

We do not pretend the case is easy, nor the issue closed, but we do seek to open it for consideration. A saving feature is that the peacemakers would be free to be patient; they need not loose the nuclear strike before long deliberation as no state beyond the initial five will soon have a large-scale, intercontinental nuclear arsenal and none will possess that capability as a surprise. There need be no agreement on the inevitability of such a strike; uncertainty about the potential act may be persuasive enough. The stakes are indeed high: it is likely that one use against an offending state would settle the issue of nuclear mass destruction for generations, while one state that succeeded in initiating nuclear war without a condign reprisal might provoke widespread nuclearization and future use.

The example of World War II is at hand: nuclear war was easily opened when there was no nuclear risk to its initiator. The political and moral future of this knotted question remains in doubt. A gradual passage to a world without nuclear weapons is to be hoped for, but it will not arrive quickly unless the international community weathers some crisis successfully. We cannot hope for the safety of a nuclear-free world without firmly arresting nuclear proliferation, and we cannot achieve that without providing credible assurances to nonnuclear nations that potential nuclear attackers can be unambiguously deterred. Such assurances of deterrence can be offered either by individual nuclear powers or by a consortium of all. We believe the latter arrangement presents fewer risks of unintended nuclear escalation.

The Common Security doctrine should not be expected to succeed immediately and everywhere. Like all difficult transitions it will have to begin as an experiment in applying the rule of law among nations. It will have to proceed by trial and error over perhaps a decade or two, during which time both successes and failures will be part of the learning process. The hopeful prospect is that common action against aggression will eventually become the canonical means of blocking wars and therefore encourage conflict resolution by negotiated agreements. Pandemic security and peaceful existence are difficult to expect within the visible temporal horizon. We can strive instead toward a world in which Common Security has rendered war a rare event, its demographic toll reduced to a modest fraction of what this well-armed and warring century has already seen.

It is easy to be pleased with the use of apparently justified economic sanctions, even stringent ones, instead of military force as an international measure to enforce the peace on a resistant state. Iraq, a land of considerable economic development under an authoritarian regime, is the most significant example since the end of apartheid rule in South Africa. But the effect of sanctions that control Iraq's foreign trade through its base in oil export has not been agreeable to the world community. In spite of extensive efforts by the United Nations to ensure supply of necessities such as infant foodstuffs and medicines, the poorer fractions of the Iraqi public are genuinely suffering, while the Ba'athist government builds palaces and maintains costly armed forces in the face of the hardships of its poor.

While there is likely to be some exaggeration in official Iraqi reports, the evidence is pretty clear. Hard times raise prices and induce shortages, not fully relieved by the rationing measures of a recalcitrant government. Those who suffer most are not the most powerful but rather the most vulnerable of Iraq's citizens.

The obvious injustice has lessened support for U.N. sanctions even though they have led to exemplary measures of control against secretive and illegal Iraqi rearming, the risk of future mass destruction as chief concern. How much the recent reaction can be remedied is not clear. Can agencies like the International Red Cross and Red Crescent Societies be given direct responsibility for allocations inside Iraq? Could they even remain independent within so heedless a regime? U.N. agencies have done much to alleviate the problems, but have not solved them. Punishment does punish, and the most injured are those nearest the margins of daily life. Perhaps free use of the media by the Security Council and its friends, including print, radio, and TV, could make the issues patent to the Iraqi public; this is an intrusive tool not yet applied. Here more experience and new ideas are needed; many events around the unprecedented Gulf War and its aftermath point to a future we do not yet grasp.

How to Get There from Here

The most daunting aspect of a Common Security regime seems to be assembling the military forces and civilian procedures to replace effectively the current system based on national forces. Experience is limited to several successful peacekeeping operations, from Sinai and Cyprus to Cambodia and Nicaragua, and one ad hoc military intervention to roll back the results of the Iraqi aggression in Kuwait. The United Nations in 1994 disposed deployment of about 70,000 armed men and women from 35 or so member states, and maintains a central multinational military staff of about 300 officers, not yet supported by all the tools they need.

A Common Security regime will eventually require the addition of a permanent and well-armed military force of similar scale to the present forces of the United Nations, and much richer resources and procedures for cases of civilian intervention. We will expand on these indispensable details in the next two chapters.

As the largest military power in the world, the United States will have to initiate diplomatic efforts designed to create a new security scheme and provide political and material support as well—the latter in the form of sophisticated weapons, logistical support, satellite and other advanced intelligence, transport, and naval and air forces essential for erecting and maintaining effective blockades. Without exemplary U.S. participation, U.N. peacemaking—not just peacekeeping—will probably be ineffective:

the coalition against Iraq was held gingerly together by major exertions of the Bush administration, pursuant to wide interest and well-financed defense of the great oil fields against seizure or implicit control. No other powerful nation has the capacity to lead the world community toward Common Security.

The United States cannot, and certainly should not, try to become the global cop who intervenes unilaterally against aggression and turbulence. On the other hand, it is in the U.S. interest to form the nucleus of an international regime that would impose stability and promote peace.

Common Security structures can be built with foresight enough to antici- pate the time when new powers will emerge in the international arena: China, India, Brazil, a united Arab world (with luck, in cooperation with Israel). In twenty years new economic powers may join the European Union and the conglomerate of smaller Pacific-rim states now under Japanese lead: Russia and China are the most probable candidates. In structuring a robust Common Security regime we cannot assume the United States will remain forever dominant. Although its role as initiator is indispensable, and its contribution of a large share of resources certainly required, future decision making should be distributed broadly enough so that the United States does not remain the central pole of the global security tent indefi- nitely. A security regime prone to collapse without continual U.S. exertions would not be credible in the first place, because for a long time it would be seen as American domination disguised as world collective action.

A century of American heavy-handedness, following to a degree in the footsteps of other dominant imperial powers, has left an imprint of mis- trust worldwide that must fade over time. If the United States makes no such changes, the price will be the slow rise of competitive power and the danger of long-deferred war. The peace we save is the peace we will share, a costly prize worth much effort. Over the long run societies that endure gravitate toward moral yet practical choices. Otherwise those nations would decline and perish. Some contemporary nations—Iraq, North Korea, Nigeria—do show self-destructive behavior. But neither the United States nor the rest of the industrialized North—nor, in fact, most devel- oping nations—deny themselves reasoned solutions to pervasive prob- lems.

With voices of isolation loud in the United States and even in the European Union, with the U.S. Congress unwilling to pay dues to the United Nations, with leaders everywhere unwilling to expose their citizens to the vagaries of U.N.-led forces, with the failures of U.N. operations in Somalia and Bosnia, the facile reaction to the concept of Common Security is to dismiss it as impractical, intrinsically ineffective, a fanciful utopian solution to an intractable problem. But we hold that this path will reopen wide again; that process has already begun in the Security Council and the office of the secretary-general.

6

On Civilian Intervention

The Common Security doctrine envisions collective *military* action as the response of last resort against aggression. Collective *civilian* intervention—ranging from diplomatic remonstrations on through sanctions, embargoes, and blockades to denial of services and later trials of specific individuals for crimes—is the alternative range of responses. Civilian sanctions with their large dynamic range, time flexibility, and broad effective applicability can be as mild or rigorous as the international community decides, can be applied all at once or gradually escalated over periods of time that can vary considerably, and can be used to counter threats to peace that range from transborder aggression to domestic violations of human rights and to nationalist, religious, or tribal civil conflicts.

But civilian intervention is in other ways much less flexible than military steps. It demands truly catholic participation by the community of nations. Military intervention can be successful even if only a small number of nations participate; but the effectiveness of civilian sanctions declines if even a small number of important states do not participate. Because of the necessity for near-unanimity, it is unreasonable to attempt to predict the efficacy of future applications of civilian interventions. Past instances of civilian intervention occurred mainly during the bipolar period of the Cold War. But precisely because sanctions were rarely subscribed to by both camps, we cannot draw conclusions about the future efficacy of such measures based on their effectiveness during the past half-century. During that time, the effects of sanctions were attenuated and delayed by the ideological competition between East and West. In instances like the U.S. unilateral embargo of Cuba, for example, they were almost obviated by the generous contributions, especially of fuel, in a kind of positive civilian intervention by the communist bloc. Thus civilian sanctions achieved their declared goals incompletely if at all. In the few cases where international participation was eventually nearly complete, as against Rhodesia and the Republic of South Africa, civil sanctions proved quite effective.[1]

Positive rather than punitive civilian intervention designed to influence policies or behavior of a target nation, including economic and military aid and treaties and most-favored trading status, have been widely used in the past, mainly on a bilateral basis. The multinational Common Security approach can use similar contributive mechanisms collectively to promote peaceful international relations. Such civilian interventions, in the form of educational or negotiating institutions, aid (for example, interest on international loans eliminated for countries that do not prepare for or commit aggression), or economic favors, can prevent conflict from escalating into combat, even discourage aggression altogether.

Both punitive and contributive (positive) civilian interventions try to achieve their stated goals by addressing nations' self-interest, implicitly assuming that leaders think and behave rationally. When they do not act based on the best interests of their nation, or when that interest is perceived differently by various parties in a dispute, civilian intervention becomes ineffective. To succeed, such intervention requires domestic transducing mechanisms that transform the pressure of international sanctions, or the allure of international offers, into national political compliance. Such transducing mechanisms can be inefficient, a fact that contributes, among others, to the long time often required for civilian sanctions to take effect. With such domestic mechanisms altogether absent, recourse to military action to force a country to comply with international norms may be the last resort.

Economic interventions therefore tend to be more effective among countries with democratic governments, among poor nations, or among those with narrowly based island economies such as Cuba, which depend vitally on exports and imports for survival. The mere threat of credible civilian sanctions could deter aggression, as well as compel aggressor states to restore the status quo ante, even submit to reparations.

Because of nations' growing economic interdependence, no country large or small can be totally immune to the effects of civilian sanctions. Vulnerability would vary from nation to nation, perhaps roughly in inverse proportion to the nation's size and the variety and adequacy of their indigenous supplies of vital needs such as food, energy, and medicines. But not even the most powerful economies could totally ignore a serious trade embargo or blockade; the penalties would eventually outweigh any benefits of aggression.

Many industrialized and developing nations alike, including the oil-producing states, import large fractions of their food supply. The United Nations embargoes food imports only rarely, but such embargoes can be a powerful, albeit cruel, tool of civilian intervention.

Embargoes of machinery, electronics, and chemical imports would be not only more humane but also more potent. Many nations critically depend on these items for the smooth functioning of their economies and their societies. Denial of such imports can have severe economic effects.

Civilian intervention is not without powerful tools, but several political, economic, diplomatic, even military conditions must exist to make them effective. Unanimity among nations in imposing the sanctions is the first and foremost requirement. And a small group of nations like the G-7 or the European Union, or even the largest, most powerful dozen nations, cannot impose sanctions; the United Nations must approve them and all must subscribe, or strife and even warfare could result. Imposing secondary sanctions on nonparticipating states could require too much economic self-denial even for the most prosperous and powerful economies.

The United Nations is the natural umbrella organization to coordinate such international functions. The Security Council is endowed with an enforcing mechanism under Article 43 of the U.N. Charter: the right to maintain and deploy a body of international troops. The Security Council is also responsible for imposing various types of sanctions. This power is stated explicitly in Article 41: "The Security Council may decide what measures not involving the use of armed forces are to be employed to give effects to its decisions, and it may call upon the members of the United Nations to apply such measures. These may include complete or partial disruption of economic relations and of rail, air, postal, telegraphic, radio, and other means of communication, and the severance of diplomatic relations."

Participation in decisions to pursue such interventions must be expanded by broadening the number of permanent members of the Security Council,

creating a new Civilian Intervention Council, or both. The political econo-
mist Lloyd Dumas has proposed a U.N. Council on Economic Sanctions
and Peacekeeping that would administer and monitor all aspects of punitive sanctions imposed by the U.N., including compensation to nations
that lose income because they participate in such sanctions.[2] We would
like to see a broader U.N. agency that not only enforces punitive sanctions
but coordinates positive civilian interventions as well.

Widening the Spectrum of Sanctions

Experience has shown which sanctions are the most effective among those
that the United Nations can impose. One is blocking air travel to and from
a country, a measure that the U.N. has enforced at different times against
Libya, South Africa, Haiti, and Iraq.

Interruption of international telecommunications, although technically
possible, has never been used as a sanction. Undersea cables and satellites
in geosynchronous orbits carry international telephone services. For example, INTELSAT, a hybrid regulatory board and international corporation,
provides space-borne telecommunications services to 170 countries; it also
"rents" excess capacity to individual nations for their domestic communication needs. Many nations or groups of nations also provide satellite
services, such as through Eurosat in Europe, Arabsat for Middle Eastern
countries, or Palapa B for Indonesia.

INTELSAT is inherently apolitical, and its operating assumption is that
the ability to communicate is an inviolable international right : the system
engenders confidence by the very fact that participating nations need never
fear that they may be denied INTELSAT services for political reasons. And
indeed, there is no precedent for withholding access to INTELSAT. The
United Nations could of course order such a step, but it is doubtful whether
the key shareholders of INTELSAT—the United States, Europe, and
Japan—would agree, mainly because such denial would cut off access to
information about the target nation. Suspension of postal service could be
another such mechanism, perhaps used to complement a trade embargo,
but facsimile technology and global computer networks would minimize
the impact of this sanction as long as telephone communications were not
severed.

But while interference with civilian telecommunications of a target nation may prove infeasible, positive intervention in the form of radio and perhaps TV broadcasts into a target nation, which would carry the news and views of the international community regarding the unacceptable behavior of the government, is clearly feasible.

Financial sanctions—including freezing credit and assets—have historically been much more effective than trade embargoes. While 85 percent of all financial sanctions have enjoyed full multilateral support—such as against Rhodesia and South Africa—only 50 percent of trade sanctions have been successful. There is good reason for that.

In 1947, the autonomous Bretton Woods organizations, the International Monetary Fund and the World Bank,[3] developed a working relationship with the United Nations. For example, the IMF agreed to adhere to any resolution passed by the Security Council. While no specific legal stipulation creates such a relationship, neither Bretton Woods organization has funded a nation deemed a target for U.N. sanctions. A future U.N. agency that managed both punitive and contributive civilian interventions could work closely with the World Bank and the IMF in fulfilling Security Council resolutions.

The United Nations maintains two indirect channels of influence on the IMF and the World Bank. First, the Western industrialized nations (Europe and the United States) exert the most influence within the financial organizations and the U.N., as they are the main financial contributors to both. For the dominant nations, the financial organizations and the U.N. represent overlapping spheres of influence. The second chain of influence is a de facto one: when the Security Council passes a resolution that might involve multilateral financial sanctions, nations pass laws requiring their banks to freeze the assets of the target country. The IMF and the World Bank therefore cannot make loans to that country because banks would be legally constrained from entering such transactions.

The imposition of credit sanctions is somewhat complicated by the existence of political risk insurance, a market begun in the late 1970s that has since proliferated enormously. This type of insurance, also known as expropriation insurance, covers the loss of an investment owing to the actions of foreign governments. The U.S. government makes it illegal for domestic underwriters to insure foreigners subject to U.S. sanctions. It is important, however, to note the existence of the Multilateral Investment Guarantee Agency (MIGA), the insurance arm of the World Bank. MIGA guarantees protection to any of its members from any of its other 106 members against the other members if "discrimination can be demonstrated." If such an insurance arrangement were made before the enactment of a U.N. resolution against any of the member countries, the insurance policy would have to pay for losses of the target country caused by an embargo or a credit freeze imposed on it. Once again, however, because the United Nations and MIGA decision makers represent the same interests, contradictory policies are unlikely to occur.

The emergence of new economic powers such as China, India, Indonesia, and Brazil early in the twenty-first century may dilute the influence of Western nations on the Bretton Woods institutions. Greater burden sharing by these members of the World Bank and IMF will lead, in spite of U.S. resistance, to greater power sharing. Until the new powers assume their rightful influence in the United Nations, the coupling between Security Council resolutions and the policies and actions of the Bretton Woods institutions may diverge. Civilian sanctions such as credit denial would therefore be more difficult to impose or less effective.

A Few Case Histories

Punitive civilian interventions have been used in the past to achieve diverse purposes. Sanctions against South Africa and Rhodesia aimed at forcing domestic change, while embargoes against Iraq, Turkey, in the case of Cyprus, and against Serbia during the recent Balkan crisis responded directly to aggression. These examples reveal the broad range of punitive civilian interventions that are possible, the complex problems they pose, the differing circumstances in which they work, and the widely varying periods of time in which they can achieve their goals.

South Africa provides a vivid example of the effects of economic, credit, and travel embargoes on a moderately developed economy with a limited parliamentary democracy. In 1962 the U.N. General Assembly passed a resolution calling upon member nations to impose economic and trade boycotts on South Africa. The United States, whose industries depended on chromium and uranium imports from South Africa, demurred. Pressure for sanctions continued in the United States, but not until 1986 did a comprehensive U.S. anti-apartheid act take effect, banning loans and new investments, trade, and exports of oil and weapons to South Africa.

Though the United States had joined the international majority, the effects of the sanctions varied. The vacuum generated by the flight of foreign industrial concerns from South Africa actually benefited the white minority in the country and worsened working conditions for the black labor force. Credit sanctions exerted more of the desired effect, capping growth of the national economy and drastically reducing imports.

Growing isolation and the need to replace imports with indigenous production actually enhanced South Africa's technological sophistication and leaders' desire to become militarily self-sufficient. The successful program to build an arsenal of nuclear weapons resulted directly from these effects. In general domestic attitudes hardened and the influence of the international community on South Africa policies diminished. Overall, however, the sanctions slowly depressed the South African economy. Together with the cultural, political, and diplomatic isolation of the country, they augured such a bleak future that no government could ignore them. F.W. de Klerk's initiatives to end apartheid were the result.

Perhaps the pariah status of the country among the Western industrialized democracies proved even more decisive than the economic impacts of sanctions. The lesson is that when applied persistently over long periods and over a wide spectrum of activities ranging from sports to weapons transfers, fully subscribed sanctions work even in cases where they exert rather modest economic impact.

The course of the civilian interventions against Rhodesia resemble those used against South Africa except for the economic impacts on third parties. In response to Rhodesian Prime Minister Ian Smith's November 1965 declaration of independence from Britain, the U.N. Security Council called on member states to withhold recognition and imposed increasingly stringent trade embargoes. But the United States, Japan, Australia, Germany, and Switzerland ignored the U.N. resolutions. Zambia and Mozambique complained of sustained economic damages since they offered the regular thoroughfares through which Rhodesia conducted its trade. In response the United Nations invoked articles 49 and 51 to extend compensatory economic aide to these two nations.

Despite Cold War–inspired U.S. meddling,[4] the measures against Rhodesia produced the desired effect. As the GDP of the country began falling owing to the sanctions (the country saw a decline of 5.6 percent in 1966 alone), the Smith government was finally persuaded to accept majority rule. In 1980 the new state of Zimbabwe emerged and was recognized by the international community. The economic sanctions had not curtailed internal economic activity but did stifle economic growth and, as in the case of South Africa, foreshadowed a grim future for the nation. Civilian intervention had required 15 years to work.

Even though sanctions against Rhodesia were imposed because of its belligerent threat to regional peace, in both this and the South African case the intervention of the international community aimed fundamentally at changing domestic policies. As such it created precedents for overriding the sovereign rights of nations and establishing the legitimacy of international civilian punitive intervention in defense of civil and human rights.

The 1974 U.S. embargo of weapons transfers to Turkey in response to the latter's invasion and occupation of northern Cyprus failed to produce the desired result because a major proponent of sanctions and the target country were interdependent: Turkey, a member of NATO, depended on the United States for military assistance, but the latter felt it needed Turkey's continuing participation in the NATO alliance to contain the Soviet Union. In this case the sanctions were also unilateral. Both factors militated against their success, and U.S. arms sales and military aid to Turkey resumed in 1978.

In the case of Iraq, its invasion of Kuwait entailed unquestioned aggression, and civilian intervention was prompt, almost universal (Cuba and Yemen dissented).[5] The sanctions encompassed most of the available spectrum and included a complete trade and credit embargo, termination of air and banking services, and a naval blockade. It is clear, however, that several factors have delayed the effects of punitive civilian intervention against this aggressor. First there seems to be only a weak link between the hardships imposed on Iraq by international sanctions and the behavior, or fate, of the government. Also, the Iraqi government had evidently anticipated the international opprobrium that greeted its invasion of Kuwait and stockpiled food, funds, and spare parts for both its industry and the military.

Those factors have lengthened the time needed to see effects from the embargo but have not denied them altogether. Food supplies in Iraq continue to dwindle and the military is slowly losing operational ability as spare parts hoarded or cannibalized run out. Iraqi industry is already at a standstill and the economy is shrinking. Gold reserves that provided some foreign currency with which essential contraband could be purchased are rapidly depleting. The circumstances tend to confirm that sanctions begin to have effect within five years. The speed of such effects seem to be inversely proportional to the size of the target nation. The oft-heard complaint that "sanctions did not get Hussein out of Kuwait and have not overthrown him" seem to reflect a lack of recognition of how long civilian interventions usually take. It is also misleading to expect sanctions to "overthrow Saddam Hussein." The sanctions are seeking changes in the *behavior* of the Iraqi government, not change of the government itself, an arbitrary ad hominem goal popular mainly in the United States.

The 1996 acquiescence of the Iraqi government to the sale of its oil under U.N. supervision to purchase needed food and medicine is a humane correction to the civilian sanctions against Iraq. It underscores the tension between the desire to achieve compliance with accepted norms of international behavior without military measures and the concern for the welfare of civilians in the sanctioned nation, especially a nondemocratic one.

Preparations for Victory by Civil Intervention

Successful application of punitive civilian interventions depends on a number of conditions. We have already identified the need for catholic participation, at the very least of all major trading nations. Such participation is more probable if the target nation is not a major economic presence in the world market; or if its actions threaten the vital national interests of the major powers, as with the invasion of Kuwait. A second condition is the existence of effective enforcing mechanisms in the participating states. The United Nations does not have customs inspectors or a central bank to apply the punitive decisions of the Security Council. Implementation of these decisions will be as effective as the enforcing organs of the participating countries. In turn individual enforcing nations may pursue economic sanctions most vigorously if that does not result in substantial economic losses for them. This is best achieved if nations observing the sanctions are compensated from a central U.N. fund for such losses. The speed with which civilian interventions will exert effect depends to a considerable degree on the economic and political characteristics of the target state. Large countries with authoritarian regimes will respond more slowly to sanctions than small states or those with well-developed parliamentary democracies.

Will U.N. members be prepared to impose secondary sanctions against nations that do not participate fully in punitive measures against a violator? Such a move could occur occasionally, but it is often politically possible for nations to focus secondary sanctions only on individual companies that violate an embargo rather than on an entire country. The same narrowly focused approach can apply to credit sanctions: rather than freezing credit and assets against a government, nations can impose secondary credit sanctions against private firms or even individuals, as is being done with Haitian military leaders and Yugoslavian banks.

Even purely civilian interventions will often require some military assistance. Blockades, even simpler embargoes, require military presence for proper enforcement: surface or submarine vessels to interdict shipping, space-borne and airborne reconnaissance to monitor land traffic, even token U.N. border guards to monitor movement in and out of a targeted nation. More intensive air oversight, as is now being applied in Bosnia and northern and southern Iraq, requires a well-organized and well-supplied force of fighter-bomber aircraft assigned to U.N. patrol duty.

The lightning success of military intervention against Iraq in annulling its aggression in Kuwait has generated the impression that U.N. military measures bring faster results than civilian interventions such as embargoes or economic sanctions. But the other example of U.N. armed intervention, Korea, took almost four years to cancel the gains of aggression.[6] Civilian interventions, then, though they appear to trade promptness of effect for absence of violence, may not always prove slower. Certainly they cost much less in life, treasure, and domestic political burden and they do not wage war in the name of peace. The potential fragility of military coalitions and domestic reactions to battle casualties also allow civilian measures to be more persistent. Domestic political acceptability, low economic costs—compared with the costs of war in casualties and treasure—and the low public profile of economic sanctions all contribute to their stability and persistence and therefore increase the probability of their ultimate success.

The painful experience of gradual military escalation in Vietnam and Korea, and the gratifying speed of success when overwhelming military force was used in Iraq, make the option of controlled escalation of military operations against rogue nations more difficult to adopt in the future. The flexibility of civilian intervention, on the other hand, has diplomatic, political, psychological, and practical advantages. Financial sanctions can be imposed initially on the government of a target nation but not on the private sector, for example, avoiding unwanted punishment of the population. If the effects of the sanctions seem to be circumvented or are deemed inefficient, they can be extended to the private sector to increase domestic pressure on the malfeasant government.

A key advantage of civilian versus military sanctions is that they can be applied against nations more or less impervious to military measures such as China, India, Japan, or other geographically or economically large states. The military forces needed to mount punitive measures against such nations would certainly be beyond U.N. capabilities. Civilian sanctions would have to be proportionate to the economic "inertial mass" of the target nation. The 1980 U.S. grain embargo against the Soviet Union in response to its aggression in Afghanistan, and the arms embargo against Turkey because of its occupation of northern Cyprus, were ineffectual not only because they were not U.N. sponsored and therefore did not enjoy catholic participation, but also because they were proportionately insignificant compared with the volume of economic activity and military holdings of the target nations. Finally, by avoiding loss of life and destruction of property in a target nation, civilian punitive interventions may make it politically and emotionally easier for a violator of international norms to reverse policy and return to lawful international behavior.

The greatest disadvantage of civilian sanctions is the uncertainty of their duration before they can achieve their stated purpose. Because the effectiveness of civilian intervention depends on so many variables and local circumstances, it is difficult to predict the onset of their effects and the probability of final success. Large developed and developing nations can adjust to civilian sanctions by accepting a lower standard of living for their citizens and stagnation of their economy for years. It is difficult to quantify the effects of sanctions in order to decide a priori the approximate needed duration. The efficacy of selective, targeted sanctions with direct and visible effects may be quantitatively measured, but partial sanctions are difficult to impose, verify, and monitor and may lengthen the wait for decisive effects.

An additional disadvantage of embargoes and other economic sanctions is the uneven hardships they cause: the poor are affected the most and the earliest, as is the case in Iraq and Haiti. Leaders of sanctioned nations have been able to use these effects for political gain, funneling effects to opposition populations or invoking "external intervention" to galvanize the population's patriotism and deflect political pressures generated by the effects of intervention on everyday life.

What's more, civilian sanctions, even when they reverse the results of aggression, do not in themselves destroy the means of aggression and therefore the capacity of the aggressor to pursue aggression in the future. Establishing self-destruction of the means of aggression as a condition for lifting the civilian sanctions removes that problem but also points out the need to define early on the terms, goals, and conditions under which the sanctions can be lifted. Just as military intervention requires the institutional procedures and logistical preparations that make it credible and therefore deterring, civilian sanctions require similar preparations.

A special U.N. agency in charge of civilian interventions, punitive and contributive alike, could go a long way toward establishing an escalating menu of sanctions to be invoked by specific political decision, not an automatic statute binding nations in advance. For political debate is the surest guarantee of how states will act, certainly for many decades to come until the Common Security system has matured.

It seems important to institute at the U.N. level some institution to maintain surveillance over civilian sanctions. The modern world has so many links of information, finance, credit, and trade that technical supervision over them is a prerequisite for success. Such supervision may arise out of regional precursors such as the various NATO and CSCE (Conference on Security and Cooperation in Europe) bodies that supervise arms-related trade from computers to chemicals, and the international financing of such trade as well. Civilian sanctions are complex and require special and ambitious study if they are to replace the gamble of war.

stressed as a phenomenon of our electronic world. The moral claim of visible tragedy is strong, and reinforced by the pleas of refugees made personal through the steady spread of technology and the growing familiarity of the whole world with far-off lands.

Indeed, on the sanctions side of the bargain the loss is clear: trade denial over a wide span (including impediments to information and fiscal exchanges) and on occasion forceful compulsion. These losses must be offset. Real gains must foreseeably derive from compliance. People are not donkeys; they see alternatives and even manage defenses (to the point of hostage taking). But gain also needs to be visible to those being sanctioned, who stand to accrue capital flow from the rich, redress of some legitimate grievances by compromise, and the common defense of all peaceable lands against aggression. These exchanges must become over time far more complex than the carrot-stick metaphor suggests, or they will not succeed, and conflict will grow to a chronic state.

7

How Much Is Enough: The Military after 2000

In this chapter we depart from our usual approach—searching over broad stretches of space and time for feasible arrangements urged by reason and nations' self-interest and permissible by objective conditions—to adopt a "proof of theory" analysis of reductions of U.S. military forces and the parallel waxing of Common Security. We hope to show that the transition from large national forces to smaller national establishments half to a third the size of their Cold War days is possible, desirable, and safe. Many European nations on both sides of the notorious, now defunct, Iron Curtain have already adopted reductions; France is the latest practitioner. (See table 7.1 for annual military budgets of seventeen selected countries.)

We hope to achieve two more objectives in this chapter with quantitative detail. The first is to outline our analytical methodology that leads us to the forces we propose: the threat, strategy, forces, tactics. The second is to forestall criticism that our proposals may appear attractive when painted in broad strokes but are not feasible when examined in their practical details.

With the inflated threats of the Cold War behind us, the United States must determine the size of its military establishment best suited to the turbulence and instability that may accompany the ensuing demographic, political, and economic changes. Along with the traditional complement of powerful allies, the nation now can count on the military forces made possible under a regime of Common Security. The fact that the United States will fight with and never against our Common Security allies is decisive in setting the sizes of both U.S. and Common Security forces. We begin with a description of what we believe will be adequately powerful

Table 7.1
Calibrating the forces: nations' annual military budgets (in billions of U.S. dollars), 1996

	Military budget	GDP	%GDP
United States	264	7,600	3.5
Russia	48	1,160	4.3
China	8.4	560	1.5
Japan	46.8	4,700	1.0
Germany	33.6	1,908	1.8
France	38.6	1,538	2.5
England	33.2	1,014	3.3
India	8.4	330	2.5
Israel	7.0	78	9.0
Iran	3.4	62	5.1
North Korea	5.3	21	25
Iraq	2.7	18.3	15.0
Libya	1.4	25	5.6
Turkey	6.8	167	4.0
Brazil	6.9	46	1.5
Canada	9.8	571	1.7
Mexico	2.7	287	0.9

Source: Institute for Strategic Studies (London), *Military Balance, 1995–1996.*

U.S. national forces and then outline the evolutionary development of the Common Security forces able to deter—or to counter if necessary—progressively more serious threats to world peace.

In the real world of today, and certainly for enough years in the future to allow prudent reconsideration, the U.S. armed forces will have no rivals in power anywhere on the globe, especially once the geography of any plausible combat is accounted for. While we want to avoid sudden changes, we do not accept as a reasonable standard the status quo—the current hypertrophied state of the military around the world. To design our policy and our forces, we must first look at those against whom we might fight, where we might fight, and how.

The bulk of U.S. military costs stem from our the large nonnuclear forces. After all, it is those forces that have actively fought several bloody wars in the fifty years since World War II, while nuclear war has remained grimly potential. We believe that the end of the Cold War between the nuclear superpowers opens an unmatched opportunity to begin a step-by-step process toward a world of nations by and large determined to keep the peace. Frequent international cooperation to gain that end, promised in 1945 with the institution of the United Nations, then all but vitiated by five decades of Cold War, can grow again. But it cannot grow well in a world armed with modern weapons at the present scale. To begin the tricky passage to a more cooperative and reasonable international order, we must reduce the three-quarters-of-a-trillion-dollar annual expenditure on arms worldwide and the deep fears those weapons nourish.

The best beginning we know is a sensible, prompt reduction of American military force, much the largest in the world and one largely designed against an adversary now in national ruin. That will send the best of signals abroad. Indeed it can also help us solve our own thorny problems here with cities, health care, education, infrastructure, employment.

Peace is the first and most precious of all the outcomes we intend; but there is a second dividend. Any prudent shrinking of military expenses will bring budget savings not of a mere $50–100 billion but real money—a near-trillion or more in a decade. Money is important, but our first question must be, is it safe to save? We propose to show that America is safer if we reduce the giant forces we built for the Cold War than if we keep them so large.

In what follows we spell out what we ought to keep and why. The prudent, fair, and humane redirection of money, physical plant, and able people is more than we can here address; the adjustment raises major problems for the years ahead. But equally it opens wide a splendid opportunity just when we need it.

A military establishment defined along mission rather than service lines seems more amenable to reasoned restructuring. The separation of U.S. military forces in particular into land, sea, and air components results from tradition as well as the differing technologies, tactics, and training each environment requires. That old partition is now obviated by experience with joint operations. The air-land battle doctrine developed in the 1970s for the defense of Europe, and the Gulf War in which land, air, naval, and space-borne weapons and systems were successfully combined, indicate that U.S. military forces may be advantageously structured by function rather than by service.

Instead of traditional boundaries, we see six distinct military functions, one day perhaps to become organized commands: nuclear deterrence; air-land battle; sea control; land-sea interface; intelligence and
space; and research, development, testing, and evaluation. This structure, even if unofficial, provides the opportunity for a "zero-base" restructuring of the U.S. military. We will examine some of the forces necessary
for these functions in some detail, but only summarize the scope and cost
of others.

We justify our judgments about various military forces by appeal to
reasonable arguments—chiefly technical, political, and economic—but
also to history. The complexity of war does not often admit reliable prediction, or wars would hardly ever begin. But conventional thinking does not
always determine the real state of affairs.

That is not to advocate U.S. unreadiness nor complacence but to insist
that we take a wide view of aims and consequences. Remember Pearl Harbor! For fifty years that stunning attack on our fleet in Honolulu has mostly
been invoked to argue the indispensability of unfailing preparedness. But
one battle is not a war. Pearl Harbor was a clear tactical triumph for the
Japanese Imperial Navy, but for Japan as a whole it was strategic disaster.
There was hardly any other way in which American force could have been
brought so quickly and so determinedly into full war. Pearl Harbor was
no Japanese success at all but rather a great American strategic victory,[1]
one bitterly won by default.

Similarly, Desert Storm's month of complete air victory in the skies of
Kuwait and Iraq may carry its own seductively false lesson. The engagement drew upon an inventory of weapons from orbit to the deep sea
designed and mobilized against an enemy far more powerful than Iraq.
The entire Gulf War theater was a "desert with nowhere for the enemy to
hide, fighting. . . no more than five days. . . casualties [on the Allied side]
counted on one hand, . . . both oil and nuclear weapons at stake . . . the
enemy [one] who will accept no compromise, and the whole . . . paid for
by Germany and Japan."[2]

We waged protracted air war against almost no air opposition; our
adversary had not one effective ally nor any sources of resupply. The Gulf
was a theater as suited to U.S. weapons as Vietnam was a disaster. Victory
over Baghdad might teach a lesson as wrong as the one we cite from defeat

at Pearl Harbor. As authors, we claim no special exemption from that sort of error, but we urge readers to reconsider with care every easy analogy.

The Proposed U.S. Military Forces by Year 2005

We outline now in broader strokes our proposals for what official reports call "general purpose forces"—those that are nonstrategic (and nonnuclear, too, as the United States reduces deployment of tactical nuclear weapons), including the major components of U.S. military forces, tanks, aircraft, and naval vessels.

Air-Land Battle

Tanks: The tank entered history late in World War I and gained its reputation for decisiveness in the battles of World War II, first in the Blitzkrieg of France, then in the Western Desert in North Africa, and finally across the plains eastward to the Volga and then back westward to the Oder.

During the last few years TV has shown us tanks in action at a few important junctures: the young man in the streets of Beijing with empty hands and a full heart facing down a tank by words alone; the line of Russian tanks with open turrets, their drivers smiling as they were given flowers in front of the House of the Soviets on the evening the 1993 Moscow coup collapsed; and the masses of burnt-out Iraqi tank carcasses strewn across the desert.

Those images carry much meaning. First of all, even with their cannon, the steel-layered creatures are not invulnerable, but they are decisive against crowds of angry citizens or even rifle-carrying troops in the open, always provided the tank crews remain loyal. The tank is itself one of the best antitank weapons, although armored combat helicopter and missile- and cannon-carrying fixed-wing attack airplanes, all armed and trained for close air support of ground combat, are the newest and perhaps most powerful enemies of tanks.

The U.S. Army and Marine Corps have plenty of tanks, rolling or stored, 16,000 by overall count. As many as 7,000 are post-1980 advanced main battle tanks. It is these heavyweights—the Abrams—that roll in our armored divisions. For performance, speed, endurance on and off the road;

for range, accuracy, and firepower by day or night; and for protection of the crew they are first-rate, at a cost of about $4 million apiece. Modern main battle tanks are to be found in large numbers only in U.S., West European, and Russian forces and in the Middle East. All armies elsewhere hold either only a few such tanks or larger numbers of much older and less capable tanks. There are two exceptions: South Korea has assembled some 500 current-model Abrams tanks, under license from the United States, and the Saudi army has bought even newer ones.

How many modern main battle tanks ought the United States to field as the decade ends? Security against the tank holdings of the so far unformed successors to the Red Army is the first gauge. Here it seems that German preparations for their own defense in Central Europe ought to guide our own. They deploy almost 4,000 top-line tanks, as good or better than our best.[3] Their NATO partners, France and the United Kingdom, together add another 2,500 good modern tanks. U.S. Army holdings in Europe have risen to about 6,500 of the best tanks, including stored replacements.

We propose that U.S.-deployed battle tanks should roughly match French or British armored forces, in equitable and prudent support. We can allot 1,200 of our best heavy tanks, each weighing about 60 tons, half of them stored but half with crews and support able and ready to fight in Europe. (We already pre-position a division's worth of heavy tanks—some 1,110—on that continent.) We can expect European preparations against a hostile Soviet bloc to dwindle rapidly as intentions and forces to the East are transformed; they reduced all armed forces by about one-third by 1995.

Since the United States between two great oceans has interests wider than Europe, we need to attend to the rest of the tank-holding world as well. In the Middle East, Iraq had the largest array of up-to-date tanks before its Gulf War losses. Larger Iran has only a tenth of that prewar Iraqi force—fewer than 500. Now the strongest Middle Eastern tank forces are those of Israel, which possesses more than 3,000 main battle tanks, and of Syria, which has close to 4,000 in a somewhat older and Russified mix.

China and India have respectively 8,000 and 3,000 tanks of older design, but their large armies and larger territories are hardly likely to be engaged by American ground forces in any invasion of Asia in the next decade or two. No nation, save Germany, France, and Britain, possibly Israel and South Korea, now has the tank forces to compare in combat power with

500 of our new tanks, and only a few even have as many tanks in total. With 500 of our top tanks deployed and another 500 in storage, allotted to face potential trouble outside Europe, we will be well prepared for any foreseeable contingency: 2,500 of our best main battle tanks will do.

Aircraft against Tanks: Air combat against tanks, heavy and light, is an Air Force and U.S. Army specialty. Newer helicopters with armor, guns, missiles, and tactics as well, specially designed for tank warfare and other close air support of ground fighting, are a priority of the U.S. Army.[4] Fixed-wing aircraft, notably the slower, sturdy, venerable, and formidable Wart Hog (A-10), using Maverick-TV guided bombs, have also demonstrated fine antitank capabilities, proverbially from the treetops.

U.S. armed combat helicopters are numerous indeed: we have about 2,200 of them, twice as many as held by the rest of NATO and high in quality. The ground-attack fixed-wing aircraft of the U.S. Air Force constitute about half of the NATO total and 30 percent more than the holdings of the ex-Soviet bloc. Since the U.S. share of antitank aircraft is so large, we propose to keep it higher than what would follow simply from the sharp reduction in U.S. tank forces.

A cut by a factor of three in our air-land battle aircraft—a dozen squadrons, say 300 fixed-wing ground-support aircraft and 700 helicopters—would maintain the present disproportionate U.S. contribution to tank war from the air. Again we would retain more than France or Britain and compare well with the present German forces—themselves surely undergoing reduction. This force will easily meet what we might need outside of Europe, since air power in the rest of the world is relatively smaller than in Europe.

Control of the Seas

Aircraft Carriers: No warship type has ever been so costly, complex, or large as the modern thousand-foot-long U.S. Navy attack carriers. The *Queen Elizabeth II* does not rival our carriers: the nuclear-powered Nimitz class, for instance, carries 5,000 men and women worldwide at 35 miles an hour. That single carrier can transport to any coast a one-ship air strike comparable to the entire air strength of a country like Canada or Denmark.

The carrier can be safely offshore yet launch attacks inland a couple of hundred miles.

The U.S. Navy at the end of 1997 operated 12 such carriers (6 of them nuclear-powered, each launching some 85 modern aircraft, including ground-attack planes, fighters, and bombers.[5] One reason we hold so many is the need for maintenance: only one-third to one-half of active carriers can be ready to move at any time. Each has its own battle group—an escorting convoy of half a dozen warships and submarines, to protect it from attack on the long voyage to action. Food, fuel for the planes if not for the nuclear-powered ships, ammunition, and missiles are brought by six fast specialized supply vessels that can replenish the carriers while under way on long wartime voyages. These ships need their own fistful of protecting frigates.

But despite this protection and support, the coming of satellite reconnaissance, of effective guided and homing antiship missiles, and of newer, quieter nuclear-powered attack subs means that carriers at sea could be quickly located and sunk, or so damaged that they could not effectively launch and receive their planes. Their vulnerability will increase slowly with time, so that they are a fading asset.

Our Navy carriers today have a purpose different from great fleet action. Their chief function is to "show the flag" spectacularly, giving implicit warning of U.S. hostile action, and also to undertake such missions as the control of straits and ports from the sea. They project American air power, both by threat of attack and by lethal attack itself, to places where friendly airbases ashore are lacking. That is plainly a path to intervention into most small countries, where air defense is not able to fend off even a portion of U.S. air power.

In the world we hope to enter there is no great reason to go it so thoroughly alone. Six active large carriers would seem plenty to retain, still an unmatched force for the free, unsanctioned projection of American power. We ought to become wise enough and patient enough to accept that in a world with a new cooperative view of security, we need not hold so much power against distant states. Perhaps two carriers might normally be posted to nonviolent missions—for instance, to rescue, supply relief, and enable evacuation under international sponsorship or even on our own.

A case might well be made for several new smaller carriers as flexible replacements for these, the biggest of ships.

Our principle that the U.S. Navy should contribute to the collective security of allies a force second to none but not one larger than any two allows a generous U.S. fleet of 30-plus destroyers and frigates beyond the 18 we assign to carrier battle groups. That implies an overall surface combatant strength of 12 cruisers, 50 destroyers and frigates, and 6 big carriers. The FY 2001 number set by the 1996 *Report of the Secretary of Defense* is 118 surface combat ships of all types. We recommend a draw-down to about 65 surface combat ships, mostly of newer types, a cut not disproportionate to that we found reasonable for the Army.

Submarines: The modern submarine powered by a nuclear reactor is the "true submersible" that realizes the dream of naval visionaries since Jules Verne. Such a ship need not refuel, peer at the sky, or breathe a single gulp of outside air for 10,000 or 20,000 leagues under the sea, circumnavigating the globe at a sustained speed faster than any other warship can claim.

The Navy now has about 75 fast nuclear-powered attack submarines.[6] For antisub and antiship action attack subs are believed to be the best of weapons, though they have almost no actual combat experience.

One major mission of U.S. attack subs was defending against Soviet air and submarine attack on the transatlantic supply and troop convoys by which U.S. forces would support a war in Europe, especially if it remained nonnuclear. That mission is now ended. Our attack subs carry fast, deep-running torpedoes effective against ships or submarines up to 30 miles away, as well as all-weather, anti-ship homing cruise missiles, some useful even against land targets 500 miles away. Surface ships are genuinely vulnerable to these fast and long-legged covert attackers at sea. Attacks on maritime commerce extend the sub's purpose. A way should be sought to modify attack submarines to allow them to slow down or stop surface ships without sinking them to support an international blockade, a sanction short of sinking ships in actual war.

It is not easy to plan a force size for these ominous ships in a more ordered world, but a proportionate cut, down to 40 of the newer attack subs (the Los Angeles class, SSN-688 or improved), should leave the active

Navy with awesome undersea combat power to guard its surface battle groups and convoys, maintain a lethal blockade, and even directly attack warships.

Overall Numbers

We next proceed to a summary quantitative description of the U.S. forces we propose to fulfill the six functions we have identified and discussed (see table 7.2). These forces are adequate to undertake six or eight Somalia-like operations at the same time, or to mount a force somewhat larger than the American part of Desert Storm. Overall they would remain more capable and more versatile than any other in the world, at a cost reduced about 60 percent from the 1992 Cold War peak—to $150 billion (in 1997 dollars). Another $25 billion must be budgeted for military pensions and retirement pay every year.

What does this money buy? About 14 percent pays for nuclear deterrence. Almost equal portions are spent on intelligence, including space activities, and on R&D, including tests and evaluation. The remaining 60 percent goes for combat forces and their full support, pay, training, and weapons. Of that amount, air-land battle claims 25 percent, sea control a little less, and forces for the land-sea interface about 10 percent. (The more traditional partition among the services finds the Navy with the largest share, almost 30 percent, the Air Force next, with 25 percent, the Army at 17 percent, and the Marines at 6 percent.)

Nuclear Deterrence: This includes land-based missiles, submarine-based missiles, and intercontinental bombers to provide the ability to launch a retaliatory strike after an enemy's first strike on the United States.

In chapter 3 we described the U.S. nuclear forces planned for the end of the century. Our table showed the DOD proposal as modified by the Bush-Yeltsin agreement, and our own proposal for still smaller forces in 2003. We estimate the overall annual cost of the strategic forces we retain at $23 billion (in 1997 dollars).[7]

We have not included the relatively small outlays for tactical nuclear weapons, since all their launchers are now dual-purpose. The additional nuclear costs hardly exceed $250 million.

Table 7.2
Numbers and annual costs of proposed U.S. armed forces (in billions of 1997 dollars)

	Number	Cost
Nuclear deterrence		23
Nonnuclear forces		
Air-land		
Active divisions[a]	5	16.8
Reserve divisions	10	5.8
Air superiority		
Active	400	9.6
Reserve	400	3
Sealift	Chartered ships	
Land-sea		
Active Marine divisions	1	1.6
Reserve Marine divisions	1	0.6
Aircraft	150	2.4
Amphibious ships	50	4.0
Airlift		
Planes	500	6.0
Sea control		
Carrier groups[b]	6	21.6
Mine warfare ships	15	0.4
Attack subs	40	5.9
P-3c patrol aircraft	260	3.1
Surface combatants[c]	47	3.6
Auxiliary ships	50	1.4
Total for nonnuclear forces		~84
Intelligence and space		19.2
Research, development, testing, and evaluation		18.0
Total		~150

a. Active divisions include 2,000 main battle tanks, 300 ground-support aircraft, and 700 combat helicopters.
b. Each group has 1 aircraft carrier with 40 primary aircraft, 1 cruiser, 3 destroyers, 2 frigates, 2 attack submarines, and 6 fast supply ships.
c. Surface combatants include 7 cruisers and 40 frigates and destroyers.

Air-Land Battle: This includes heavily armored troops, tanks and artillery, armored helicopters and planes fit for ground attack, free to keep to the air because of our air superiority overseas, as our own shores are not vulnerable to ground attack.

Ground Forces: The U.S. Army is planning to reduce the sixteen divisions it maintained in 1991 to 10 divisions after 1997. (An Army division at wartime strength totals 17,000 men and women and has a choice of ample supplementary units.) Marine divisions provide troops over and above this Army force.

We see no real use for standing ground forces so large. We propose for the first decade of the next century one fully armored division, one airborne division, and six independent brigades at roughly 6,000 soldiers each, two with two main battle tank battalions each, the others with a mix of lighter units. We would also retain two armored cavalry regiments—faster, lighter, smaller armored units, intended for easier mobility and reconnaissance; the present plan deploys three of these in 1997. Overall this force would deploy about 500 main battle tanks in Europe and a similar number in other theaters. An equal number would be stored, ready to enter battle.

Overall U.S. strength would stem from flexible, mobile ground forces equal to about four and a half divisions with a heavy core of almost two full armored divisions. Active Army forces would number about 180,000 persons.

We suggested a reduction in tactical air strength to accompany the deep cut in ground forces. Yet we would retain air strength greater than proportionate to our residual ground forces to reflect the size, technical prowess, and superb training of American aviation—a special contribution to the overall security of our allies.

The Air Force plans to deploy in 1998 51 combat squadrons of fighter and ground-attack fixed-wing aircraft totaling 1,000 planes, counting only the "primary aircraft authorized" for the units. The present active U.S. Air Force tactical aircraft support an army of about 16 divisions. Because we have proposed to cut that ground force by a factor of 3.5, we would recommend tactical air strength of about one-third the 1993 size. These would include 18 squadrons armed with the newest aircraft (stealthy F-117s), top-of-the-line fighters (F-15s and F-16s), and the tough old battlefield A-10s.

Sea Control: Big aircraft carriers with many surface escorts and nuclear-powered hunter-killer submarines can be used to clear sea lanes and impose blockades.

Among all the services, the U.S. Navy now receives the largest share of the military budget, if only by a small amount. So much of that expenditure is centered on the 12 active aircraft-carrier battle groups that our stringent reduction in that force alone will sharply reduce the number of warships for conventional warfare. The 1997 DOD plan calls for an amazing 12 carrier battle groups, clearly implying major commands for senior flag officers. Surface support now provides six warships for each carrier at sea, mostly cruisers and frigates. Twelve antiair and antiship missile cruisers (most nuclear-propelled, some the newer but smaller gas-turbine *Ticonderoga* class) and eighteen of the newer antisubmarine destroyers (*Spruance* or newer) and frigates would amply furnish surface escort for the fleet of six carriers we propose. To the surface ships in each battle group we would add two nuclear-powered attack submarines.

The auxiliaries needed for the blue-water aircraft carriers are called underway replenishment groups. We require 3 such groups, 5 fast specialized ships in each. To these first-line combat support ships we add 15 more, to make up half of the 60 combat support ships of the DOD plan. Many other support ships fulfill a wide range of purposes even farther from combat, including sub and destroyer tenders, floating dry docks, hospital ships, and others. The FY 97 plan sets such support ships at 40; we propose to keep 30, pending more detailed study. New naval shipbuilding would all but end; by 2000 the Navy would operate not the 420 active ships and subs now planned but about 160. The navies of the remaining world total about 400 ships, half held by NATO European nations, the other half by Russia, China, India, and Japan.

Naval air strength is principally held as carrier-borne combat air wings. We propose not 12 but 6 such carriers. Again the naval air strength might be held somewhat higher than proportionate to the carrier number, for these powerful units can be based on land runways as well. The early 1990s' count of 620 active naval fighter and attack aircraft (56 carrier-borne combat squadrons) can be reduced stepwise to 20 squadrons, or about 240 planes. The 1998 count stands at 35 squadrons with 440 aircraft.

The large land-based force of long-range maritime patrol aircraft, aimed mostly against submarines but of general use for surface surveillance on the high seas, may be retained near full strength in this world of surprises. About 250 active turboprop patrol planes (Orion P-3s) can survey most important ocean areas along with the patrols of our maritime allies. By the end of the next decade many of these will be replaced by long-endurance, unpiloted reconnaissance aircraft.

Land-Sea Interface: This function relies largely on light, mobile over-beach infantry, including Marines, with small helicopter carriers and special transport of all kinds and nuclear-powered submarines with accurate cruise missiles prepared for assault and interdiction operations work at the shore. This command is the one that would be most responsible for supporting increasingly frequent U.S. participation in international forces both peacekeeping and punitive, as well as in tasks of humanitarian assistance.

The Marines by tradition and origin are an elite ship-borne force, prepared to land on distant shores. But the Marine Corps has grown so large, with its own air force and moderately heavy weapons, that it now has a fourth of the strength of the entire Army. No operation of quick forcible entry at this multidivision scale seems in the cards; in Iraq, a landing by two brigades was ostensibly prepared but ended as an offshore feint, without a landing.

The Marines have a special near-shore capability in green water gained through long devotion to ambitious over-the-beach amphibious operations. One Marine Expeditionary Unit (MEU) numbers about 2,500 men and women, with ten tanks and artillery batteries, half a dozen V/STOL (vertical or short takeoff and landing) attack aircraft, and thirty helicopters. We now have a dozen or more helicopter and assault carriers, able to carry and land an MEU with its armor at any beach. These allow well for the more flexible, speedy, small-scale responses the future appears to require from the Marines, whether sent across the beach for interventionary attack or for less belligerent missions such as the operations in Somalia.

That ability seems worth preserving. Even if entry by force becomes as rare as it should, Marine abilities allow quick action through inadequate seaports. We propose enough Marine forces to compose up to a dozen distinct MEUs, which might be grouped as needed with some help from naval aircraft carriers and prepositioned shipping. This would be a long-overdue reduction of Marine forces from the present number—almost 200,000 strong—to about 50,000 persons, or one augmented division and its needed air support. Those forces would retain about twenty-five of the present sixty-five amphibious warfare ships, mainly the newer ones.

The two Marine Expeditionary Brigades (each containing six MEU) would enjoy appropriate air support if given 150 fixed-wing combat air-craft (including their 40 unique vertical-takeoff Harriers) and a similar number of gunship and transport helicopters. These can be borne by the helicopter carriers as well as by the big carriers.

Intelligence and Space: This includes the National Reconnaissance Office, which procures military satellites, the present Space Command, with its early-warning functions and orbital worldwide monitoring, and the Central Intelligence Agency, Defense Intelligence Agency, National Security Agency, and all the other information-gathering agencies.

The costs of military information gathering, including a valuable segment in orbit, are more or less secret, split up among agencies so that no official budget figures are stated. Of course an informal estimate does exist, recently more and more confirmed publicly.[8] We use that as a basis for our proposal.

The largest single item in this budget ($13 billion in 1997 dollars) now goes to tactical intelligence—the reconnaissance aircraft, radio monitoring, and dozen other organized activities that bring short-term battlefield information directly to combat forces. We cut these more or less proportionately to the reduction in the size of the forces themselves.

A similar sum is now divided between diverse military satellites and the signal-intercepting and -decrypting organization, the National Security Agency. We recommend only minor cuts in these expenditures to retain a strong global flow of information (the United States cannot examine other nations' books!). Smaller intelligence agencies serve the uniformed services, the DOD itself, and other departments of government. We can reduce these a little. The celebrated CIA—estimated to cost one-tenth of the present intelligence-gathering total—we propose to cut by half, to curtail doubtful covert operations everywhere.

The result overall is to decrease the total cost of intelligence, including space, from the surmised mid-1990s sum of $29 billion to $19 billion (1997 dollars) by the early years after 2000. All these items deserve study by an independent commission with access to the secret record; serious consideration should be give to sharing of intelligence and its costs with our allies and with the United Nations.

Research, Development, Testing, and Evaluation: The Directorate of Defense Research and Engineering, the Defense Advance Research Projects Agency, and the laboratories, test ranges, and facilities of the current armed services and the Department of Energy would take responsibility for weapons research and development required by the five other military organizations listed above.

R&D on new weapons, nuclear and conventional, has provided the U.S. military with an unsurpassed technological edge on the battlefield and an undoubted deterrence to nuclear aggression. In 1999 weapons research, at almost $40 billion, will take 60 percent of all federal R&D funds, of which $34 billion will go for development, testing, and evaluation of new weapons.

Forty years of such investments have paid off: U.S. arms are now technologically superior overall to what an opponent could deploy even a decade in the future. The race to stay ahead can now slow down. At $15 billion a year, military R&D would nearly equal the sum of all current U.S. civilian R&D programs except those directed toward space. This amount would still total almost ten times the investments in military R&D of Germany and Japan combined. After canceling further work on the V-22 Osprey tilt-rotor aircraft and the Sea-Wolf and Centurion submarines, and such R&D programs as the ballistic-missile defense program and the planned upgrades of existing advanced aircraft, ample funding will remain for communications, electronic countermeasures, and surveillance-and-attack systems to keep American arms immune to obsolescence. Basic and applied military research can continue at present levels ($5 billion in 1997 dollars per year) and still leave ample funds for the advanced-technology and technology-base programs.

The Men and Women of the U.S. Armed Forces

The French words of military art—*materiel* and *personnel*—are abstractions, but the weapons systems and the devoted human beings organized to make and use them are real. Reducing the size of military forces means ending jobs and switching the careers of many people who deserve better. The nation ought to do all it can for them as part of its transition from Cold War to peacetime. How far America will compensate them financially, offer them new access to education and training, help them find other jobs, perhaps even assign some to new civil duties while still on the military payroll we cannot say without detailed study. Retirement costs of military personnel will plainly increase sharply as well.

The task of economic transition would surely be a major issue and an inescapable cost ensuing from large reductions in military budgets. On the national agenda will stand a new imperative: to offer young men and women from every background at least as hopeful an entry to civilian careers as the armed forces have provided for many, from new privates to the chief of staff. Once again opportunity opens along with cost.

An important part of our armed forces is the part-time military, the reserves. These include those who train and serve part-time in organized reserve units and also those who fill out incomplete active units when called; many of the latter are recently retired military personnel. The reserves serve in all branches of the forces and perform a wide variety of tasks. Most familiar are the organized units of the Selected Reserve, which include the Army and Air National Guard.

We have included the cost of reserve forces in the outlays we foresee. In 1992, the peak year following the rearmament efforts of the 1980s, those outlays amounted to about $20 billion of a total of some $270 billion. The reserves will probably increase rather than fall in cost and numbers in the years just ahead, in part as a transition for those who leave military careers and in part as insurance against the chance that the country will again need to field a larger military. A large stock of tanks, guns, aircraft, ships, and much besides will also have to be carefully stockpiled and cocooned, again as lasting insurance. Such an effort will demand expert and enduring care, including prudent training and maintenance of specialized skills. Such changes need not happen overnight. The average rate of reduction we foresee is remarkably similar to past rates of decline from peak force sizes, both in the mid-1950s after Korea and in the early 1970s after Vietnam.

We estimate that the number of uniformed full-time women and men in the U.S. armed forces can be reduced by two-thirds, from 1.8 million to 600,000 as the new century opens. We would cut the reserves much less, from about 1.1 million to half that number. The Department of Defense now employs more than a million civilians mainly in administrative and service jobs. That number can be slowly reduced to no more than 400,000 to reflect proportionately the reductions in armed personnel.

The defense industries that develop and manufacture the multitude of weapons and systems for war, from the simple M-16 rifle to the nuclear aircraft carrier and the nuclear-tipped intercontinental ballistic missile, have grown in the past half-century to employ at Cold War's end in 1992 over 3 million people. The frenetic pace of weapons development and production can now slow to a rhythm more suitable to peacetime.

In shrinking the size of the weapons complex, we are mindful of the need to maintain a competent industrial base that can support future military exertions if they ever become necessary. The technical know-how and worker skills that are embodied in naval nuclear reactors, for example, have to be nurtured, as will the special knowledge incorporated in the amazing fighter aircraft as well as one assembly line for their production. One shipyard in the nation must be reserved for constructing and more importantly maintaining, repairing, and upgrading the Navy's surface and submarine vessels. The electronic wizardry of communications, intelligence gathering, and electronic warfare must be amply supported. But duplicate facilities and technological ebullience in the field of weapons will have to be eliminated.

Totally novel weapons do not appear necessary to us: "giant" and "insect" battlefield robots have some promising potential uses, but their effects will probably be at the margins. "Nonlethal" weapons, the latest fashion of the military-industrial complex, are mostly in the realm of humanitarian science fiction: the countermeasures are easily imaginable. Using nonnuclear devices to generate electromagnetic pulses that disrupt battlefield electronics may spark a spiral of countermeasures and counter-countermeasures, an intriguing prospect for engineers. Advances in electronics and materials will spawn smaller, faster, more reliable versions of existing systems. Large vehicles, planes, surface vessels, and tanks will become increasingly vulnerable; countermeasures will lessen this vulnerability but the larger systems may no longer prove decisive in battle. However, barring a drastic change in the level of threat to U.S. security, only modest levels of funding will be necessary to support the development of such new weapons.

Overall a peacetime military, well stocked with weapons more advanced than any other nation's, does not require more than a quarter of the industrial infrastructure that provided it with the latest weapons. Perhaps no more than three-quarters of a million workers, engineers, and scientists should remain occupied with weapons for war.

These changes are difficult, but not dauntingly so. The present job shortfall in our economy is some 8 million; cutting the U.S. military effort will over five years add half as many more. The burden is lightened by the immediate federal budget savings and the lower cost of investing in civilian jobs compared with those of the defense industry.

We cannot believe that the only way to employ skilled Americans is to build more billion-dollar nuclear submarines when we already hold a hundred for which we now have little use. Neither are international arms sales a sensible alternative. The United States sold $22 billion worth of advanced conventional weapons to less-developed nations in 1992—a threefold increase after 1989, reflecting increasing pressures from the weapons industry. The sales were about $20 billion in 1997, a marked reduction from the 1993 record of $60 billion.

We believe that Americans along with the citizens of the other nations who live with some degree of comfort and safety will have to replace mutual fear with mutual aid or enter into a fiercely unstable world. To produce a stable world most persons, even the myriad of poor—many here in the wealthy United States—need to see some path that promises them safety, justice, and well-being ahead. Those few nations who will not embrace the promise must encounter high barriers against their efforts at violent international change, barriers that will be well guarded by the many.

We have perhaps five decades to nourish that outcome from our present world of bitter division and its implied conflicts. Certainly violent conflict will not disappear, nor will military forces, but both need to dwindle greatly in scale so terrible weapons of mass destruction can sleep.

Great hope comes from one fact: the economic, technical, and human resources now sequestered annually in the unproductive world of arms amount to the major part of a trillion dollars a year worldwide. In nature and size these resources are capable of bringing profound change to the lives of most of the world's people. Among those billions of dollars and wide-ranging talents a working solution to our acute environmental and human problems rests, not less—and with good judgment not more—than one long lifetime ahead.

Military Forces for Common Security

Here we calibrate the size of the world's forces needed for Common Security based on the missions we would expect them to undertake as reliance on them to safeguard peace increases during the coming decades.

Peace is at risk from old habits and new tension worldwide. Adversaries, be they political, tribal, or international, still tend to resolve their conflicts by resorting to the time-honored method of combat. The unshackling of Eastern Europe and the Caucasus from Soviet bonds, the proliferation of efficient weapons among African tribes, Iraq's 1990 aggression—all contributed to breaches of what the world hoped would be undisturbed peace after the Cold War. The need for collective action in the form of a Common Security military force has become increasingly apparent.

These pragmatic considerations provide a framework within which we now define the parameters of practical Common Security military forces— their size, combat readiness, availability, response time, and provenance.

What missions should Common Security forces, organized and commanded by the United Nations, be able to carry out to maintain peace? We count six:

- Deter preparations for aggression.
- Deter aggression itself.
- Reverse any gains achieved by aggression.
- Punish aggression.
- Perform peacekeeping and peacemaking operations (such as separating combatants and monitoring cease-fires or elections).
- Undertake humanitarian missions.

While the last two missions can always be achieved with the consent of the affected nations or parties, the first four cannot be accomplished without such permission under any circumstances.

Preventing preparations for aggression, or aggression itself, requires that any potential aggressor believes that such preparations will be detected in their early stages, and that there exist both the political will and the means—military or otherwise—to foreclose successful aggression. To reverse or punish aggression may very well require military forces that can range in size from a competent brigade to a multidivision force not unlike the one assembled to end the Iraqi occupation of Kuwait in 1991.

The last two missions listed above, in contrast, well practiced by U.N.–led forces for several decades now, require the familiar lightly armed contingents capable of self-defense in an uncertain but usually not hostile environment. From these overall requirements derive the need first for monitoring and intelligence-gathering capabilities and second for combat-ready military contingents that can stand in the way of aggression anywhere in the world in a timely manner.

We propose three layers of preparedness embodied in forces of different size, readiness, and provenance:

- A standing 5,000-person quick-reaction force ready to be deployed within forty-eight hours.
- A division-sized force of about 30,000 soldiers, composed of several brigade-sized national contingents, that could be fully deployed within a month.
- An estimated multinational expeditionary force of half a million, comparable to the one that pushed Iraq out of Kuwait, that would require four to six months to be fully deployed, logistically supported, and combat ready.

The relatively long response times of the second and third tiers of a Common Security force will not diminish the deterring effect of such forces provided that the United Nations has clear institutional structures and operational procedures to assemble these forces, as well as the a priori political mandate to do so when triggered by well-defined contingencies. Furthermore, as we argue here, the United Nations will need to establish permanent logistics, intelligence, command, control, communications, and personnel and training capabilities to support any of the three tiers of forces. U.N. contingents operating in Bosnia and Somalia lacked adequate logistics and command, control, communication, and intelligence (C3I) and thus produced disappointing results. Our proposals for Common Security forces and preparations are intended explicitly to eliminate these weaknesses and to approach the performance standards of NATO.

The Quick-Reaction Force

The permanent quick-reaction force, a ready brigade of 5,000 soldiers, can consist of volunteers from any of the U.N. member nations enlisted for a fixed term, much like the legendary "Legion Etrangère" of the French Republic, though without its mercenary air.

The quick-reaction Common Security force would be divided into four light infantry airborne/air assault battalions. These in turn could be stationed in various parts of the world to speed deployment time. The battalions would typically need close air support by national air forces earmarked for U.N. use. Air strikes would be necessary because the small size of the reaction force and its transport would preclude the use of heavy mortars or tube artillery for fire support. The latter types of indirect firepower would come into play only once the larger, less-mobile rapid-deployment force arrives to supplement the quick-reaction force.

Finally, a helicopter air wing would be necessary for transport and fire support. Usually a two-to-one ratio of transport to attack helicopters is sufficient. Larger equipment such as humvees can be transported along with supplies once a drop zone is secured.

In the first years of its existence, the quick-reaction force might be stationed and trained at U.S. military bases or the NATO base in Germany now used for training multinational forces. Scandinavian, Indian, Russian, and Chinese bases might also be called upon, to maintain the multinational nature of the force from the start.

The quick-reaction force would transport most of the supplies it needs. Soldiers would carry shelter, ammunition, and food to the first assembly area in the country of operations. Equipment and supplies to supplement them would be air dropped. Because of this, a lane of air superiority would have to be opened along with a secure drop zone, used for medical evacuation as well. Such an effort would require far fewer people than needed to open up and secure a land route through potentially unfriendly territory. If the reaction force moved to further objectives, airdrops would also be more cost-effective than a land route requiring fuel for trucks and escorts.

Pensions and benefits for the members of this force who made it their career would be funded by the international community. Otherwise, a pension supplement dependent on the number of years of service would be added to the soldier's national military pension and funded internationally. Maintaining, training, and amortizing the force's weapons would cost the United Nations about half a billion dollars a year. Donated equipment and spares would reduce the cost by about 10 percent. On the other hand, frequent training exercises involving the use of combat aircraft would eliminate such savings.

The Second Force: A Rapid-Deployment Division

The second-tier Common Security force will be a division-size rapid-deployment contingent of approximately 30,000 troops. It would consist of three infantry brigades (with armored personnel carriers), an aviation brigade, division artillery, and support groups of mechanics, scouts, communications and intelligence personnel, antiaircraft defenses, logistics, and transport equivalent to one more brigade. Thus the rapid-deployment force will be operationally self-sufficient, except for close air support. A wing of aircraft consisting of air superiority, close air support, electronic warfare, and AWACS (airborne warning and control systems) planes will be needed to support this rapid-deployment force. The air assets can be contributed by a militarily advanced nation, probably the United States or Russia. Similarly, transport, both air and sea, for this rapid deployment force will have to be provided by a large military power, preferably the United States, that possesses the necessary landing craft and very large transport planes. The cost of using these support forces in training or war can be subtracted from the annual U.N. dues of the country that provides them.

The rapid deployment force can have its central base in a country such as Canada, Mexico, or Sweden, preferably near a large-capacity all-weather seaport. The base will hold all the heavy equipment of the force, its logistics, communications, C3I, permanent headquarters, and training facilities. It will be permanently staffed by a skeleton crew augmented by elements of the support brigade.

Each of the three infantry and aviation brigades could come from a different U.N. nation and serve for three years: one year in training at the base and two years on standing readiness within their nation. Although each brigade will come from a different nation, they could be chosen each time from nations that speak the same (or similar) languages. For example, an English-speaking rapid-deployment force on a three-year tour could consist of brigades from any of the following nations: United States, United Kingdom, Ireland, Australia, Canada, India, Pakistan, or the Scandinavian nations, which have obligatory English as a second language. A Spanish-speaking force could similarly consist of Mexican, Spanish, and Argentinian brigades. Several such combinations are possible, so nations will not have to contribute a brigade more than once every dozen years or so.

To ensure that a rapid-deployment force is always available, the three-year tours of each force will overlap. During the third and final year, the brigades of the next group of contributing nations would be transported to the base and begin training. When traveling for rotation, the troops could be transported by ship or surface transport, but they would be deployed by air when on a U.N. mission. The rapid-deployment force's armor, heavy weapons, and equipment will be transported to the theater of operations by ship, allowing deployment within about one month.

With proper transportation, the unit could be able to enter combat within less than forty days: seven days of preparation before departure, less than twenty-one days travel time by sea for the heavy equipment, and seven days of preparation once in the area of operations. A small naval transportation fleet made up of fast sea-lift and roll-on/roll-off ships will make this unit truly a rapid-deployment force. Although the ground troops can be in place in a few days, transported by air, the armored vehicles must be taken by sea.

Equipment for the force will have to be replaced every fifteen to twenty years, either by U.N. purchase or donations of materiel from member nations that would meet performance and standard specifications. While the weapons and associated maintenance facilities would be located at the central base, material like ammunition, spare parts, lubricants, and other logistical support can be stored at several points around the world for faster delivery to any theater of operation.

The quick-reaction force would maintain 250 main battle tanks to provide heavy firepower without hampering mobility. Approximately 1,000 armored personnel carriers would be needed, for mobility and protection for the soldiers. Late models of American, Russian, or German armored personnel carriers may be suitable; a unit of this size will require the most efficient, maneuverable, and powerful vehicles. An air wing of less than 100 American or Russian helicopters would be necessary for close air support and reconnaissance. Accompanying these would be more conventional helicopters used for logistical support and medical evacuations.

As with the quick-reaction force, national air forces would have to furnish close air support. There are two reasons for this. First, a permanent international air force would be logistically unwieldy. Air fields would have to be established as permanent bases and large amounts of fuel and ammunition stored there. Second, an international air force would necessarily consist of older models of aircraft. A naval air wing from a U.N. member country would be more effective if the operations of the rapid deployment force were within the range of its aircraft. Otherwise, militarily advanced members of the United Nations will have to contribute one wing of land-based aircraft.

The base proposed for this force could help rectify a serious problem that has beset U.N. operations (other than the unusual U.S.-dominated Korea and Iraq operations.). U.N. forces have not maintained intelligence gathering and information processing operations nor adequate joint training of national contingents. The result has been a lack of coherent integration of troops and weapons, no prepositioned available supplies, no logistics base and trained logistics personnel, and therefore no permanent stocks of materiel, equipment, heavy weapons, transport, or ammunition. Even more serious is the lack of reliable command, control, and communications infrastructure and the absence of clear lines of command. A permanent training base that will contain the headquarters of U.N. forces, with the accompanying C3I, logistical, and maintenance commands, can go a long way toward remedying the widely acknowledged shortcomings of U.N. military operations: lack of integration between field commanders and logistical and transport resources, decoupling between U.N. headquarters in New York and forces in the field, and inactivity of the military staff committee established to provide overall coordination and control of U.N. military operations. The base offers the locus for establishing a permanent U.N. military nucleus, a general staff responsible for organizing, training, equipping, and commanding the quick-response and rapid-deployment contingents. Planning, logistical preparations, and the liaison function between the political authorities at the U.N. in New York and the

U.N. military will also be tasks for this permanent staff, drawn from all services of several nations. Experienced officers distinguished in their national armies could make second careers of service in the U.N. military staff.

The permanent military staff could be divided into four or more commands: administrative, logistics, planning, operations, and C3I for a total of 400 personnel.[9] Many of the operational difficulties now experienced by the 70,000 military personnel serving in a dozen U.N. missions could be addressed by the proper functioning of such a general staff.

Readiness status could be determined by international events. There is no need for the entire unit of this size to be constantly on alert. Should the quick-reaction force be activated, the rapid-deployment force would automatically go onto alert. This level of readiness could also be achieved by a command from the U.N. Security Council.

We estimate the cost of maintaining the rapid-deployment force in active status to be about $3 billion per year. That sum includes the costs of maintenance and operations at the base and of training and transporting the brigades from their countries of origin and back. This amount represents less than one half of 1 percent of yearly global military expenditures. Each nation should pay the United Nations on the order of .5 percent of its national defense budget. As the Common Security regime takes hold and allows cuts in national military budgets, the proportional cost of the U.N. forces may rise closer to 1 percent a year.

The Largest Common Security Force

The U.N. military response to Iraq's transborder aggression into Kuwait provided a measure of the largest force the Common Security approach should be prepared to deploy. Iraq, in the summer of 1990, by a combination of circumstances unlikely to be duplicated in future situations, presented an unusual military presence. The country was rich because of its oil holdings, and the United States and other NATO nations had provided substantial support for Iraq's economy and military buildup. In addition, Iraq's military was hardened by its war against Iran. We can think of few nations outside the G-8 group of industrial and military powers that could duplicate these circumstances: Iran perhaps, a United Korean peninsula, Turkey, and India, currently in no way hostile.

The forces arrayed against Iraq by January 1991 give a sense of the scale of an effective U.N.-sponsored force.

• *Ground forces*: nearly half a million men and women in 55 brigades, with over 3,000 tanks, nearly 2,000 guns, and multiple rocket launchers and 600 attack helicopters.
• *Naval forces*: 111 U.S. naval vessels, including 6 carriers, 2 cruisers, 7 frigates, and 3 destroyers, plus 79 more ships contributed by 15 other nations for a total of 190 vessels.
• *Air forces*: at least 1,870 aircraft, 1,396 of them land-based, in January 1991, at the beginning of the air campaign.

This was a very large force but a conceivable goal for U.N.-led Common Security arrangements, and a reasonable intermediate between the multimillion-person forces of the Cold War era and the 50,000-strong rapid-deployment force. When the smaller forces we propose accumulate a satisfactory record of prompt and successful Common Security operations, such a large force could prove possible, but perhaps it will never become necessary.

NATO provides a ready model for assembling such a half-million-strong force: each of two or three large states like the United States, perhaps Japan, Russia, India, and China could contribute two to three divisions each, while another ten or so states could contribute one division, earmarked to join specific missions as needed. In peacetime, these forces would be under national command, just like those of NATO allies. Multinational forces have performed well in past engagements, as was the case in Korea and during World War II. Commanding such a force would require the Security Council to appoint a commander for the specific occasion and the temporary expansion of the basic staff of the Common Security forces that we proposed in the context of the rapid-deployment force.

Independently of the size of a U.N.-ordered Common Security intervention, whether military or civilian, naval units, both surface and submarine, will be needed to enforce blockades by intercepting with nondestructive actions vessels steaming toward the blockaded nation. In instances of military intervention, naval transport and naval air may be needed to carry troops and materiel to the theater of operation, or to support ground operations from the air.

The Gulf War experience has shown the utility of ship- or submarine-launched long-range accurate cruise missiles for tactical and strategic strikes.

On occasions in which the Security Council has authorized such strikes, U.S. naval units with their accurate sea-launched cruise missiles could perform the mission for the United Nations.

Air power will also be needed to support U.N. Common Security measures both civilian and military: support of ground operations, transport, and enforcement of blockades; show of U.N. force; intelligence gathering both as a deterrent to aggression and during military operations; monitoring of the terms of agreements and of embargoes; and strategic and tactical bombing during military opposition to aggression. Since the United Nations cannot afford an air force of its own, the necessary air support will have to come from either a joint air force from several nations when operational circumstances allow it, or, especially in the case of a rapid-deployment force, a mixed air wing of a single national air force, preferably from a technologically advanced nation.

Space-borne intelligence gathering, reconnaissance, and monitoring seem indispensable capabilities for a U.N.-based Common Security regime. Needed missions would include verification of compliance with international agreements, reassurance to nations as inducement to enter agreements, surveillance as a deterrent to nations preparing for aggression or violating agreements, advance warning of aggression to trigger preventive diplomacy, evidence of aggression as a basis for adjudication, cease-fire monitoring, and communications services in support of U.N. civilian and military interventions and during natural disasters.

These services could be provided by a U.N.-owned satellite or fulfilled by data regularly delivered to the United Nations by nations possessing space-borne reconnaissance satellites, including the United States, France, and Russia. This information could take any of three forms: processed photographic images, open-channel real-time telemetry as received directly from satellites, or real-time imagery interpreted by the provider. A large number of operational and legal problems will have to be resolved in any of the three instances, but the U.N. Committee on Peaceful Uses of Outer Space (COPUOS) has the experience to do so given a mandate from the Security Council. While a U.N.-owned and operated satellite and ground monitoring station would cost a few hundred million dollars and guarantee impartiality and prompt access to data, we believe that the Common Security regime we propose would be adequately supported by national data provided to the United Nations.

A fully functional and effective Common Security structure led by the United Nations and supported by a majority of large and small nations can be in place by the end of the century. As it gains experience and credibility, its applicability will grow, but its capabilities will have to be carefully balanced. On the one hand, it should have the capacity to oppose a determined and militarily prepared aggressor. On the other, the Common Security forces cannot grow to appear as a threat to the independence of most nations, thereby inducing them to increase their national armed forces. An armaments race between individual sovereign states and the United Nations would be an ironic outcome.

A limit on the size and level of activity of the Common Security forces will be their cost. We estimate that the current $4 billion annual cost of U.N. military operations will increase by a factor of seven or eight to about $30 billion as Common Security matures into a reliable and well-prepared regime. This is a small fraction of global military expenditures, but comparable to the defense budget of Germany. The knowledgeable *SIPRI Yearbook* estimates that by the year 2000 global military expenditures will total $700 billion, three-quarters stemming from the industrial North.[10] Measured on this scale, the cost of Common Security looks not only manageable but inconsequential, especially when one recalls that the military resources of the North will support, not oppose, the forces of Common Security.

We suggest direct proportional taxation of the international arms trade, carried out by national means, levied on both exporters and importers, the bulk of the proceeds to go to the international authorities. The Security Council or its surrogates would have specific power to exempt individual buyers. This procedure appears to offer an incremental method to stem the flood of arms that is an artifact of the military hypertrophy of this half-century without singling out particular purveyors.

The Rules of Engagement

Confusion within today's U.N. military operations—and the resulting widespread disenchantment with them—has resulted from ill-defined rules of engagement. Though we recognize the political disadvantages, we propose a rigid set of rules for applying U.N. military force. We divide the threats to international peace into three categories.

First is the unambiguous forcible crossing of international frontiers. Here we believe the United Nations should use appropriate elements of the triad of forces we have already described to oppose such aggression decisively. This nonconsensual use of force should be applied automatically when triggered by transborder aggression. The mission of the U.N. forces would be to restore the status quo ante bellum, to exact payment of reparations from the aggressor to the victim state, and, depending on the circumstances, to permanently reduce the military capabilities of the aggressor to a point that it could not support future aggression without prolonged, and therefore visible, preparations.

Second, we recommend that the United Nations should continue the largely successful practice of inserting peacekeeping forces into situations where a cease-fire has already been agreed upon and the presence of U.N. forces has been requested and agreed to by both belligerents. Such missions are often intertwined with local needs for relief and multiple forms of humanitarian aid that the various U.N. organizations, along with other nongovernmental organizations, have frequently provided. This, the most basic function of Common Security arrangements, is already established as acceptable in a limited set of broadly agreed-upon circumstances. It is the foundation on which the international community can build successive layers of Common Security institutions.

The third class of belligerence is active civil, tribal, ethnic, and religious conflicts. The Cold War had spawned a number of such conflicts from Vietnam to Nicaragua, Salvador, Cambodia, and Angola. After the collapse of the Soviet Union these wars were, in many cases, successfully calmed with the help of U.N. mediation services and peacekeeping forces. We advocate continuation of that practice.

There remains, however, a class of such conflicts that merits more detailed analysis. Civil strife, as in Bosnia, Somalia, or Mozambique, poses a sharp choice between strictly observing the sovereignty of nations and violating it by intervening for humanitarian reasons. Organizing the world community as an assembly of sovereign nation-states and operating according to the principle of nonintervention has maintained stability and order, if not always peace, for almost two centuries. But how rigid should adherence to nonintervention, even by multinational forces, be in the face of gross and massive human rights violations such as the tribal massacres of Rwanda? How much should individual human rights be sacrificed to world order? Although the question invites the use of moral criteria for its resolution, we see the need for a pragmatic approach. The rules of engagement should be based on what demands the aftermath of intervention will require of the United Nations, and of the nations participating under its rubric in such intervention.

We believe that the United Nations should avoid military entry into such unresolved conflicts. Intervention can take the form of civilian measures such as embargoes and cutoffs of services where a government in power is fomenting strife by severely violating civil and human rights. Civilian intervention against neighbors assisting rebellious forces opposing a democratically elected government are also conceivable. The United Nations should offer to mediate conflicts like those in Yugoslavia, Somalia, Mozambique, or Burundi, and to alleviate human suffering, but not to intervene militarily. Usually exhaustion and economic collapse will force the opposing factions into reconciliation, as was largely the case in Lebanon.

We believe that such principles of intervention have real and practical merit. They provide a framework for action or inaction that member states can explain and defend to their domestic constituencies. The principles address the fears and consequent objections of numerous small and developing and underdeveloped nations who fear that U.N. military forces will facilitate intervention by the major powers into domestic affairs. The principles erect a clear-cut barrier against nations hoping to acquire wealth by aggression. While in the industrialized nations surplus wealth depends only weakly on land and its resident labor, in many underdeveloped nations a pragmatic cost-benefit analysis of war against a neighbor may well lead to the conclusion that a few thousand or even tens of thousands of casualties may be worth the forceful acquisition of arable land or other natural resources. A categorical U.N. commitment to deny such gains, by military intervention if necessary, can eventually lead to the reduction of military forces in recidivist nations and thereby allow parallel reductions of defensive preparations in neighboring states. National economies would benefit without exception.

Finally, we enter less familiar ground: armed intervention into civil war within a single state, without mutual consent of the parties to the conflict.

Since civil wars are frequent within states, and in this time of failing states are even increasing in number, a peaceable future requires realistic procedures to deal with their occurrence. External intervention into civil conflict is as old as the state system. States have always held the option to enter—or even to foment—a civil war, and then to join it. But always the intervenors were states with policy gain as goal, from the entry of France into the American Revolution on the side of the colonialists in the 1780s to the sudden Soviet move into Kabul in 1979. One side of the conflict had served the foreign interest, if only on the desperate principle of statecraft that the enemy of my enemy is my friend. (Mr. Churchill avowed that he would say a few words of praise in the House of Commons even for the Devil, should that Power come under Nazi attack.)

Border transgression by an attacking state is a rather well-defined act for most states. Outsiders can thus agree on the event first, and then weigh their own appetites for intervention. But civil war is far more intricate. It may or may not have a local habitation, and its scale and vigor vary widely. Few states escape all serious internal conflict; most states at some time harbor residents who combine against the interest of the state. Some states indeed have arbitrary borders that enclose disparate populations and tribes, whose definition was at best imposed during the flow of history. Whole mutinous cities have been destroyed by artillery (in Syria, for instance) without external response, and clear majorities have been humiliated and denied their most basic claims of citizenship, as in the Republic of South Africa after World War II, with long-delayed response from the most powerful states.

Violent actions are everyday events, even large and protracted ones, and parting civil disorder from civil war is no easy matter. It is plain that any decision to intervene abroad in defense of—or against—some existing state is a highly political matter, among the gravest of foreign policies, especially if the scale is not small. A world with colonies old and new, with long histories of previous conflict, with renewed conflicts that arise from causes ethnic, religious, economic, or vengeful, is not a world in which U.N. obligations are easily imposed on reluctant states far from the events.

The community of states will have to decide the nature and scale of intervention into civil war as it has done in the past, where single states, allies, or even states on both sides (as in the civil war in Spain) entered with force. Since the mutual action we foresee requires the consent of many states and blood payment by some, the overall consensus is less likely to be a narrow reflection of single national interests than in the past.

Almost every state welcomes international bodies that would permit intervention to help preserve a nation's territory, for some day it might need that help. But by the same general argument states are apt to oppose intervention against state powers in civil conflicts. Since that structural bias exists, states are likely to join such actions only when their security is high and the case at hand is egregious, involving massacre or prolonged suppression of large groups on invidious grounds, or brazen breach of faith in international agreements. Even then the powerful will not be punished easily; a modest-sized, determined, and well-armed state in a favorable strategic position, like that of Serbia, will draw less-than-adequate opposition from its neighbors. In the case of Bosnia, the stakes were set too high, even with the emotional display of unhappy Sarajevo on TV, and neighbors rested easier near a new Croatia and an old Serbia than next to a Bosnia that might naturally enter an alliance with Islamic powers.

We therefore entrust the international intervention into civil conflict to common and not statute law, letting a U.N. body, perhaps a standing committee of the General Assembly, examine each case on its shifting political merits. Only a wide spectrum of political responses can satisfy the interests of the states, and only occasionally will appropriate military action be taken.

8

Everyone Wins

World Economy

By almost any measure of economic activity, physical or fiscal, consumption or capital, by most measures of public health and by some of welfare—including gross product, food harvests, fuel use, urbanization, death in childhood and life expectancy, even participation in primary and higher education—the world economy (and its wastes) has increased during this century by a factor of a dozen. The size of the world economy also grew during the century before, though by a much smaller and poorly known factor.

But it must be emphasized how intensely uneven is economic activity around the world. Even the two largest and richest economic powers—booming United States and recessing Japan—account at century's end for more of the world's annual product than all the countries put together that lie outside the circle of the industrialized rich. (We have allowed for the next few years of fast growth in China and for the built-in uncertainties of such comparisons. China is still an outsider, but changing fast.) The production of the two most active lands is shared among only 0.4 billion citizens; ten times as many live in the nations we call the poor. All rich countries together account for about three-fourths of global product, though their residents add up only to a fifth of all humans. The poorer countries, where nearly four-fifths of the 6 billion dwell, manage with only a quarter of the global yield. The distribution of economic activity is evidently askew by almost an order of magnitude. It is unlikely that this will change without a steady transfer of economic growth from today's rich lands to the poorer ones.

Yet it is not inequity alone that planners, diplomats, and simple citizens must attend to. The numbers have physical meaning as goods, tools, and action. If the poor continue to emulate the rich as best they can, the world standard of living will rise to much higher levels, already patent as a goal from Rio to Kuala Lumpur, from Ulan Bator to Luanda. There's the rub! If the 8 billion people (up to 10?) of the late midcentury to come, say in 2050 or 2060, are to enjoy a per capita income in any way comparable to (if still well below that of) the average person in the well-off states today, the planetary economic yield will have to increase substantially in a lifetime. It is naive to consider such desired rates alone, as though it were all a matter of intent on paper, like the promise of interest written on the face of a bond. What counts is fulfillment. Not even vigorous bacterial growth can manage its fixed relative rate of increase for long, and certainly the products people seek—food, shelter, clothing, health, knowledge, and some of the diverse amenities of a (fortunate) citizen of the affluent countries—do not grow unattended. This world is still a world of atoms, not of bits or pulses. Atoms do not increase at all in number; to serve human purposes they must be cleverly shuffled and organized by the apt expenditure of both human and physical energy.

The world of 2000 opens with a much higher level of goods and of heads than the world of 1900. The United States now produces about $7 trillion of goods a year, and the whole world about $25 trillion. To triple that sum is daunting, and almost surely implies both a high input of resources and substantial transfers even in the rate of economic growth itself from the rich world to the poor, neither task a simple matter. What should we look for in the next decades? Is there a trend to equity?

Note that determined China anticipates passing U.S. total production in twenty-five years, thus to become by a modest margin the world's largest economy. That hoped-for economic prowess would still be divided among four or five times the expected U.S. population: an economic power but with a large majority of rather poor people. (The U.S. economy will surely not grow from its high level at a pace approaching China's.)

The initial question is the estimation of the shortfall that will still remain in a generation between the median well-off citizen at present and the real future of the poor. Equity is at most a goal; the plausible outcome is widely recognizable improvement. In short, we aim to create the conditions for real hope, but that hope cannot be based on simple extrapolations of economic growth everywhere. Development must pass from mere potential to a dominant trend outside the now-rich world.

To understand the task ahead, we need to apply what we know and can foresee of national and international organization, of human effort, of new and existing technology, and of the necessary input of natural resources. We need an era that remains substantially at peace. The motivation for our plans stems from a simple truth: the earth's atmosphere and waters, the future floods of emigrants and travelers, and the torrent of information flow link us increasingly across all the seas and climates.

Security through Economic Engagement

The last decade of the twentieth century is a time of multiple transitions. The bipolar confrontation that spawned the Cold War is yielding to a resonance of common interests among influential nations. And overall international relations are undergoing gradual transition from the traditional zero-sum approach of conflict resolution to a more enlightened win-win approach. We are moving from a state of imminent nuclear catastrophe that could have involved the entire Northern Hemisphere and parts of the South to a less ominous state in which only sporadic nuclear terrorism or even a limited nuclear exchange maintain measurable probabilities of occurrence. Finally, the species as a whole is undergoing the demographic transition to a nearly plateaued global population by the second half of the twenty-first century.

To support the transition from the condition of periodic large-scale wars with chronic regional combat to a new state of stable if not universal peace, we have proposed the eventual elimination of all nuclear weapons and the formation of Common Security forces, a tool for attentuating combat and creating conditions worldwide that permit gradual reductions of national military forces. We hold our proposals practical while recognizing that their implementation requires change in the ways nations traditionally pursue their interests. Political thinking will also have to undergo transition from a zero-sum to a win-win approach.

It is not realistic to expect that the Common Security regime can become and remain effective in keeping peace overall in a world of deep divisions and unmitigated competition. An additional tool is needed to meld a permanently stable and overall peaceful humanity. In this chapter we propose such a hopeful tool, Common Development, which we believe is necessary (perhaps not sufficient!) to achieve long-standing security for both the United States and other nations. It is a third element that complements our earlier proposals, and completes the cooperative system of international relations now accessible to humankind.

The United States has two fundamental requirements for national security. These are the physical security of the continental United States, including Alaska and Hawaii, and the worldwide protection of genuine national interests worldwide. Major elements of our global interests are safe and uninterrupted access to foreign oil supplies over the next several decades, to markets for our products and investment opportunities, and the assured toleration of some measure of political influence worldwide.

The continental United States can be threatened by nuclear weapons carried by long-range ballistic missiles or air-breathing craft, bombers, or cruise missiles; by terrorist acts; by unwanted immigrations; and not least, by a wide spectrum of possible environmental changes. Our global complex interests can be threatened in many ways. Political instability and local wars elsewhere can reduce U.S. opportunity to invest and block access to favored markets and raw materials, especially oil. A depressed global economy can reduce international demand for our products, creating unemployment at home, and prompt trade wars with other industrialized (and soon with some developing) nations. Against such threats, military force has ever-diminishing effectiveness at ever-increasing cost. The world cannot be made to work better by force, and what the United States and the other industrial nations of the North need is a stable world that works predictably and consistently better for many.

If a new national security doctrine of the United States were designed to reduce, even rectify the *causes* of instability, political tension, and local wars, our interests *and* our economic security would benefit. Religious fanaticism, ethnic conflicts, tribal wars, stubborn nationalism—all contribute to turbulence in world affairs today. But, we believe, the core cause of present and future instability is the huge asymmetry in prosperity, opportunity, hope, and security that persists between the industrialized First World and the developing and less developed countries wherein dwell at least 85 percent of the current population of the Earth.[1]

The exhausting political and strategic confrontation that has played itself out after half a century of futile military exertions has left the great world powers with their common interests opened to collective pursuit. National frontiers are more and more transparent to trade, investment, information, even to migration. In this new environment the old U.S. national security doctrine, anchored in containment and nuclear deterrence intended to defeat the doctrinal expansionism of a military superpower, is now irrelevant if not detrimental. The new challenge is how to establish order, stability, and dominant peace over the longer term. The new U.S. national security doctrine, in whatever detailed form it may emerge, can now be based on the win-win strategy rather than on the zero-sum game resolution of conflict by combat that required the Cold War military mobilization. This shift in the central security paradigm presupposes the expansion of what constitutes a politically acceptable menu of actionable options, a shift in the boundary conditions of national security policy. The reassuring simplicity of armed strength as the bloody single guarantor of that security is inapplicable for both the near term and the longer-term future. To other changes we must add a new factor brought about by the elimination of artificial barriers: hugely expanded international trade, $5 trillion worth in 1995, and the even more phenomenal expansion of international investment that reached $5.5 trillion in the same year.[2] The computer-based symbolic movement of the fiscal tokens of capital has now reached a rate of about $4 trillion *per day*, a speculative, perhaps transient, case of superfluidity.

Combined, trade and investment are fusing domestic with international economic affairs, introducing a new policy amalgam that joins domestic economy and therefore local politics with international economic policy, national security policy, and foreign policy. The United States is certainly not alone in this sea change. All the nations of the industrialized North are experiencing the same tendency to view national security increasingly in terms of economic interest rather than ideological dictates or the requirements of national sovereignty.

The Security Policy to Come

We would look for three elements of a coherent new U.S. security policy during the next decades. First is the maintenance of well-designed and powerful American military forces, albeit not at the present hypertrophied levels of the Cold War, whose annual costs now exceed the military budgets of the rest of the world put together, and whose structure and size are not matched to present threats. A more suitable force can be well paid and well prepared at about 40 percent of the annual cost of the Reagan administration's peak defense budget, or half the 1996 sum of about $260 billion. That step could save the United States alone $450 billion by the year 2002. Second is the adoption of consistent support for effective Common Security forces, ready and anchored within the United Nations, to inhibit aggression, and so permit commensurate reductions in national military budgets worldwide. Third is the initial implementation of Common Development aimed at reducing steep gradients in prosperity, security, and hope across national frontiers. In the long run that will lessen the need for and so limit the magnitude of Common Security forces.

Each of these three elements of the new U.S. security policy we propose will take its own time to reach maturity, but all can be initiated simultaneously to become mutually reinforcing. Reductions of U.S. and other military budgets return immediate savings that can be devoted to supporting both Common Security and Common Development. Such reductions will not command much support in the United States without ready and proven Common Security forces able to complement national armies against most transborder aggression. Realizing the savings requires assembling a reliable international security force, a task that could take the best part of a decade. Similarly, Common Development will have to persist for a generation to show steady results, but its hopeful success along the way will make Common Security requirements manageable and the reduction of national military budgets politically easier.

Just as U.S. foreign aid was an important component of containment doctrine during the Cold War, so it is a central aspect of the new policy of engagement we advocate here. Over the years the United States has contributed about 15 percent of the total foreign aid extended to the South and about 25 percent of the costs of U.N. operations. A tripling of the amount of aid the United States offers now, from about $8 billion to $25 billion a year, would maintain the U.S. contribution to a policy of engagement at about 15 percent. President Clinton's call on Congress "to support the institutions that the United States founded" was an apt reminder of the responsibilities but also the opportunities open to this country. The $25 billion is a small amount in absolute terms, and even smaller if compared with the enormous costs of attempting to maintain peace by force in a world expected to nearly double its population within the next generation.

The difficulty inherent in making this fundamental shift in U.S. security policy is more temperamental than it is practical. So far U.S. policy has been one of attempting to impose our national views and interests by military or economic coercion. (Vietnam has proven an inadequate lesson.) Consequently, defense and foreign policy are seen more often than not in confrontational terms, the win or lose imperative of the zero-sum game. Instead, we propose here a security policy that is inherently cooperative, a fundamental conceptual shift difficult to embrace.

Hopeful signs of a more benign, cooperative, win-win approach to international problems are apparent in Europe, as exemplified by the reach of the European Union nations toward agreement at Maastricht, and in the United States, as signaled by its endorsement of the North American Free Trade Agreement, the latest provisions of the General Agreement on Tariffs and Trade, and favorable U.S. trade agreements with China and Russia—the latter moves sound policy in spite of their ambiguities because potential difficulties with these two very large nations could never be resolved through military confrontation.

The shift from containment to engagement, and its mutually reinforcing aspects, Common Security and Common Development, will have to begin with a systematic and widespread analysis and public debate of the necessary actions, their costs, and their myriad implications, with the participation of government agencies and departments, philanthropic foundations, the university community, and professional associations.

Current levels of foreign aid and foreign investment will not prove sufficient to stabilize the economies and societies of the developing and underdeveloped world while the population tide crests. Turbulence and instability are already discernible in many parts of that world owing to large-scale internal migrations from the countryside to the dynamically growing urban centers. Cairo, Mexico City, Istanbul, Calcutta, Shanghai, São Paulo, Jakarta—all face exploding populations, deepening squalor, and growing manifestations of political extremism and discontent bred of despair. In Africa, the tribal strife that stretches from Liberia through Nigeria and Zaire to Sudan and the horn of Africa is the most visible symptom of deepening economic difficulties, exacerbated by the peaking population increase in Africa. Tutsis and Hutus slaughtered each other in Rwanda not because of an ideological divide, not owing to a tragic history alone, but because 8 million people were trying to survive in a country the size of Vermont. The migration stream from the Mahgreb and the nearer Muslim and Slavic neighbors into the affluent European Union nations is a milder manifestation of the same pattern of socioeconomic stress.

Even without causing open warfare, steep geographic gradients in opportunity, prosperity, and hope can disrupt the formal orderliness of a world of distinct states by the motivation of mass migrations from the less advanced economies to the more prosperous and stable. The northern littoral of the Mediterranean receives a constant stream of furtive immigrants from its southern shores; the sharp cleavage between the northern and southern shore of the Mediterranean may be in part the remnant of the long rule by the Europeans (see table 8.1). On the other hand the slowness of recovery and the antique institutions in some North African states continues more than fifty years after the end of colonialism there. The United States is the final destination of opportunity for Mexicans and those from the smaller states of Central America. Turks, Poles, and Yugoslavians stream into Germany and socially conscious Sweden. Even Greece, half as rich as the other European Union states, has attracted hundreds of thousands of Albanians since the fall of the Iron Curtain. It is an old, recurring phenomenon. From the fifth century onslaught of the rootless nomads onto the fecund lands of the Roman empire to Iraq's latest aggression, war or mass migration have been the ready route for leveling economic gradients. The conquest of land and resources remains today the leading cause of war among those less-advanced societies of the Second and Third World that depend on domestic agriculture. Perforation of national frontiers between industrialized and nonindustrialized societies by means of *illegal* immigration is a relatively novel phenomenon that creates serious disruptions, yet also suggests a hopeful mechanism for gradually smoothing prosperity gradients across such frontiers.

The scale of dislocations caused by the demographics of developing countries will become too great to be contained by armed opposition,

Table 8.1
The Mediterranean gradient

	Spain	France	Italy	Greece	Morocco	Algeria	Tunisia	Libya	Egypt
GDP/per capita × 10³ in thousands	12.2	23.0	17.8	10.1	1.1	1.5	1.8	9.5	0.69
Specific density	249	327	601	332	332	351	262	255	1,877
Life expectancy	79	78	79	79	65	68	68	63	63
Infant mortality	7	7	7	8	68	55	43	68	80
% Literacy	96	97	96	95	44	62	67	76	51
Unemployment	16	10	11	8	16	30	15	2	15
Inflation	3.6	2.1	3.9	8.2	6.1	15.0	3.7	7	5.4
GDP growth	2.1	2.7	2.2	1.5	11.2	1.5	3.5	-3.0	2.0
Pop. increase	0.2	0.5	0.1	0.4	2.1	2.3	2.0	3.5	2.3
% GDP military	1.5	3.1	2.2	4.8	4.2	4.0	2.0	5.1	4.5

Source: Compiled from data in the *UN Handbook of International Trade and Development*, 1995.
GDP = gross domestic product; specific density = population per unit *arable* land; life expectancy is in years; infant mortality = children per 1,000 who die under one year of age; literacy = percent of population that can read; unemployment and inflation are percentages (in 1992); GDP growth and population increase = percent of increase over the preceding year; % GDP military = percent of GDP devoted to the military budget.

especially since arms can serve both sides. We see that the affluent North has a thirty-year grant of time from the beginning of the twenty-first century. During that time the North needs to implement a new global security policy that addresses the core causes of instability and war. In the case of the United States, this positive policy, if it is to prove effective, must assume the catholic character that the denying policy of containment achieved during the Cold War. During that period not only foreign policy but also commerce and industrial policy, education, even interstate highway building were pressed into the successful pursuit of containment and its awesome complement, nuclear deterrence. A similarly integrated national policy will be needed in the pursuit of engagement, the doctrinal underpinning of Common Development, now that the end of the Cold War has rendered containment meaningless.

Asymmetries can be reduced to mutual benefit at a small fraction of the cost of maintaining them by military force, through Common Development. The European states of the Common Market have succeeded in this approach rather convincingly in only a few decades, and the nations of the Pacific Rim, led by Japan, offer confirmatory proof despite recent stormy economic conditions. Foreign investments in Taiwan, South Korea, Singapore, Hong Kong, and Indonesia have elevated their productivity—and thus their economies—markedly, but their increased demand for imports has augmented Japanese prosperity and power as well.

This decision to help the laggard by investing in unity and stability is not at all new. The laissez-faire abstention from government concern with the welfare of classes far removed from power was broken sharply in the second third of the nineteenth century during the regime of Bismarck. The tentative social welfare of that time has a certain continuity in the regimes now usual in Western Europe. The reasons for this shift were many, but the coolest view is that the future of stable governance seemed more easily and even cheaply secured by a modest sacrifice of income by the well-to-do than by force and persuasion alone. Carrots were added to sticks.

Until the mid-eighteenth century, prosperity was associated exclusively with the possession of either fertile lands or useful raw materials, or the geography (passes, rivers, ports) and social organization that supported successful trade. Starting with the Industrial Revolution, power and wealth flowed more and more to the technologically sophisticated. As the twentieth century ends, science, technology, and industry are the dominant agents that determine the place of a nation in the First, Second, or Third Worlds. Thinking anew is rapidly becoming a necessary part of work in the First World as a source of surplus wealth. The immigrations from the less to the more industrialized countries suggest the systematic long-term effort that would relax the economic gradients that threaten world stability and peace. Rather than have the workers of the Second and Third World come to the industries of the North to improve their standard of living, technology and industry can be transplanted into the less prosperous nations. Unlike land or indigenous raw materials, technology and industry are portable, and the wealth derived from them can benefit both recipient and inceptor nations.

This is the conceptual basis of our proposal for a policy of Common Development. We define it as the long-term systematic and deliberate effort by the governments of the industrial North to improve the standard of living, security, and hope of developing and underdeveloped nations while exploiting the North's comparative advantages in technology, inventiveness, and high productivity to provide products to predictably expanding markets. There is one caveat: that decreasing the overall asymmetry between North and South should not create local socioeconomic asymmetries in the societies of developing nations. A gradient between privileged and poor made steeper by inflow of investment and the opening of a developing nation to world markets can generate domestic instability and civil strife and may thus obviate the purpose of Common Development. We therefore do not believe that Common Development can occur spontaneously, driven by market forces alone. It is doubtful, for example, whether market forces alone will address problems of education, health, infrastructure, clean water, housing, public transport, and population control. These will require outright attention and support from Northern nations.

In the Muslim lands, oil-producing nations funnel aid for similar ends through fundamentalist movements. This process is ideologically driven, creates adherents for fundamentalism, and so presents a challenge to Western influence in nations like Turkey or Egypt. Ideology, though, can be a poor guide for aid, and in the U.S. experience, a failed one: during the years of containment policy, U.S. aid was meted out along anticommunist lines, often ending not among the intended recipients but among dictatorial elites or U.S. businesses, since at least some of it was "tagged," intended only to finance the purchase of U.S. services or products. This is one of the key reasons that U.S. aid to underdeveloped and developing societies after World War II failed in many, but by no means all, instances. Aid is now misunderstood in the United States, suffering from bad publicity; but even though it is unfashionable with Congress and the uninformed public, it is an essential, albeit small component, of Common Development.

The agenda that we suggest is intended to reduce gradients of prosperity, security, and opportunity but not to directly address potential environmental problems. We believe that drastic action to preserve and restore environmental integrity will have to yield priority to improving the lives of people worldwide. The two are often interdependent in many parts of the underdeveloped world, but environmental deterioration is rarely the *cause* of human misery, at least for the present. For the past half-century, the dominant agenda was to avoid a catastrophic nuclear war that could threaten the very human survival on this Earth. The next third-century should be devoted to improving the human lot on the planet. Once the great majority of the human race is provided with adequate and properly distributed food, energy, education, health care, and security from anomie, war, and oppression, then humanity can turn, in the second half of the twenty-first century, to the urgent task of environmental melioration. We do not advocate present neglect of the environment, nor do we imply indifference to the real threats we face in that arena. We hold that on balance it is world peace and the human welfare that undergirds it that take priority. *We cannot hope to address overarching environmental problems in a world riven by war and instability, which will consume the needed resources.*

In fact, we consider Common Development to be a necessary effort that will condition the response of developing and underdeveloped nations to heed the exhortations of the industrialized North to safeguard the environment. Unless the South is engaged in a mutually advantageous relationship with the North, its environmental policy will be hampered by justified obduracy. As we explain in succeeding chapters, it will not be practically possible to meet even partially the expectations of the cresting populations of China, India, or Indonesia in an environmentally benign way without vigorous participation and support by the industrial North. Developing nations will have to be engaged in a compact of environmental responsibility with the North; coercion does not work now and won't work in the future as the South sheds its weakness. It is doubtful that the market forces alone, at least ab initio, will address the need for environmentally responsible investment practices in developing and underdeveloped nations. Here once again, specific aid initiatives can generate local incentives, in this case for investing in environmental protection.

The potential returns in cheaply maintained security for the North, and the formation of huge markets in the South, driven by the demographic transition there, for sophisticated products and services, suggests the wisdom of prompt action by the U.S. and other Western governments in working to establish a Common Development regime.

The Time Is Now

Just as American resources and will were the bedrock of containment, so is the role of the U.S. government essential to the success of an engagement policy and Common Development. American leadership and resources (money, expertise, institutions) are irreplaceable for the formulation, organization, and implementation of the new security policy. The old policy and the new are comparable in scale: by the end of the Cold War, containment cost over $450 billion per year in direct military expenditures alone for the NATO alliance and Japan. In the United States domestic, trade, educational, defense, and foreign policies were all linked in support of containment. Internationally alliances were formed, institutions established, and common practices agreed upon by the Western nations and their allies in pursuit of this end goal. Common Security and Common Development exertions will have to be of comparable magnitude and coherence. Containing and eventually exploiting the explosive results of the peaking demographic transition in the nonindustrial world will require economic, political, diplomatic, and organizational determination on the scale and with the commitment elicited by anticommunist containment.

The U.S. government, together with the governments of other industrial nations, will have to make the hard "economic triage" choices and set priorities, goals, time constants, and limits in implementing Common Development. Choices will have to be made between the most promising nations—such as Poland, Thailand, Mexico, and Egypt—and the largest and most demanding lands—including Brazil, India, Pakistan, and Indonesia—and between the developing and less-developed countries. The U.S. government has to be prepared to coordinate the actions of the private sector, the Bretton Woods financial institutions, and nongovernmental organizations. Finally, the U.S. government will have to provide leadership in establishing international mechanisms to coordinate, manage, monitor, and evaluate the implementation of Common Development, in conjunction with international organizations such as the United Nations, the European Union, and the Organization of American States.

An initial policy of Common Development intended to raise the standard of living for the bulk of the people in Second and Third World nations could cost somewhat more than $260 billion (1997) dollars per year, over a generation. Ab initio, at least three-quarters of that amount would have to be provided by the developed world, through governments, the independent sector, and the multilateral financial institutions. This is a large amount of money indeed, but comparable to the $300 billion-per-year cuts in global military expenditures now possible with the end of the Cold War.

It is that very comparison that shows Common Development to be fiscally possible. The comparison, however, seriously overestimates the overall cost since Common Development itself constitutes a *security* policy. It is a policy that would focus mainly on regions of potential instability and armed strife, and so can be expected in the longer run to draw down still more the global cost of military readiness.

The tripling of U.S. foreign aid that we recommend, from $8 to $25 billion a year, represents only a deposit toward the overall cost of the new security doctrine, itself a sum much smaller than our current investment in armed force. In later chapters we will show in more detail why the U.S. government's participation in the Common Development approach appears affordable. Even if all of the additional funds were to come from the national security portion of the budget, it would withdraw less than 5 percent of current U.S. military expenditures. That would certainly prove a prudent investment if Common Development could reduce long-term international conflict and instability. Foreign aid in the form of civilian technologies—communications, transportation, health facilities, small-scale agricultural equipment, and biotechnology—could supplant U.S. foreign military assistance programs, which now cost over $10 billion per year in the form of free transfer of weapons. Since the United States manufactures both weapons and civilian equipment, the shift would not affect adversely the employment picture in the United States, though it will in time demand a new mix of products.

Optimists and Pessimists

As promising as the effects of a Common Development policy may appear, serious questions remain about its practicality. For example, does the political vision, wisdom, and will needed to implement such a policy exist in the North? Are circumstances in the South broadly conducive to the successful introduction of knowledge and technology for economic development? Is the commonality of benefits resulting from Common Development recognized in both worlds?

Pessimistic thinking can be invoked in the cases of the subcontinent of India, Central Asia, even South America. Endemic corruption and poorly functioning bureaucracies in Central and South America can be invoked to conclude that conditions in these regions are not conducive to aid and technology transfer. Take Egypt: the United States has been granting $1–2 billion a year in aid to Egypt since the Camp David accord, yet Egypt posts a literacy rate of only 48 percent and a per capita GDP of just $720 per year, the lowest in North Africa. Bureaucratic indifference is stifling; Islamic fundamentalism is rising; those movements eschew science and technology anyway. Here is an example, the critics of Common Development would claim, of a hopeless case for which such a policy could do little. Since many vital industries in developing nations are nationalized, investment opportunities there for the private sector of the North are limited: one more impediment to transferring industrial and managerial expertise to these countries for the purpose of advancing economic development by furthering their industrialization.

The pessimists' dim views of domestic conditions in many developing nations are not without foundation: bureaucracy and corruption are indeed present in many nations but, as the news media have been informing us for the last two years, so are they in Italy. Yet Italy, now the fifth-largest industrial state in the world, has still managed to achieve one of the highest per capita incomes in Europe. In Greece bureaucracy thrives, but during the past fifteen years of association with and help from the European Union the per capita income has increased steadily. Israel, with most of its industries nationalized, has made exceptional economic progress even without optimal use of the multibillion-dollar annual aid from the United States and elsewhere. Muslim nations like Turkey, Malaysia, Indonesia, and Iraq have embraced technology and developed active industries; the Iraqis even managed to come close to attaining the nuclear holy grail, a nuclear weapon. The Pakistanis achieved it. Stereotypes used indiscriminately to support arguments in favor of inaction and the traditional militarist approach to national security obscure opportunities for more promising, more farsighted and more benign international policies.

The United States has a long tradition of humanitarianism and a century-old direct involvement in international affairs. Neither Bosnia nor Somalia threaten the United States or offer economic opportunities, yet the swift transmission of images from there to our living rooms has step by step obligated U.S. involvement.

All the events of our time are visible today on television: war and famine, suffering, courage, and leadership in all the world's troubled corners. The compelling flow of images is taking its place next to politics and economics as a powerful determinant of U.S. policy—and not only U.S. policy—worldwide. That no man or woman is an island swiftly becomes less and less a metaphor and more and more a description in a tight-linked world. The broadly shared humanitarian impulses of the American public coincide not only with our national security but also with our economic interests in many regions of the world: Asia, Russia, China, and South and Central America can develop into immense potential markets for U.S. high-technology goods and services. Their prosperity and stability are the most certain guarantees for global peace and U.S. security.

Neither continued indifference nor armed violence, no matter how sophisticated, will work much longer. It is too late for their inhumane simplicities in this interactive world, with high-tech skills in every latitude, fast, easy trade, one common atmosphere to breathe, and a televised view of the fate of human beings everywhere.

The Immediate Challenge

How to structure and coordinate aid and investments on a long-term basis, and how to relate them to local requirements shaped by the activities of the for-profit sector and economic plans of receptor nations, is the central challenge of Common Development policy. On the one hand, efforts by actors in the inceptor nations uncoordinated with the economic policies and realities of receptor nations will result in inefficiencies, waste, and disenchantment with the entire attempt at Common Development, in both North and South. On the other hand, the notion of attempting to coordinate tightly the extended process of promoting international security through development and industrialization in the Second and Third Worlds over several decades and several continents appears wholly impractical and unattainable, even unwise. Short of a world government—a distant and probably undesirable prospect—there appears no single corpus of international decisions, actions, or regulations that could guide the application of Common Development policy along a wholly self-consistent, maximally efficient path.

However, if all the participants accept the principles and fundamental assumptions of Common Development, coordination can emerge from a process of trial and error. Probably Common Development will initially be a quasi-chaotic process, its trajectory bounded by the imperatives and self-interests that the various actors will bring to the process. National governments will seek security, stability, peace, and prosperity for their populations; the developing world will seek a fairer redistribution of wealth; domestic constituencies will demand fairly shared prosperity; the nations of the industrial North will require, at a minimum, no erosion of *their* standard of living; the private sector will focus on profit.

These imperatives can bound a converging search for effective Common Development practices provided that the societies of the industrial states recognize that the price of stable peace is a limit on one-sided economic and military power, and that their prosperity cannot increase ad infinitum, either promoted or protected by armed force. The private sector's imperative, the continued realization of profits, if not their unbounded growth, can be fulfilled in the context of Common Development. We believe that we propose here a policy that allows market forces modulated by a coherent and consistent international security imperative to rectify the asymmetries that cause turbulence. The hopeful conclusion is that the for-profit sector can and will contribute to the stochastic focusing of the multitude of actions and decisions required for a Common Development security policy. The private sector would be motivated to participate in efforts to improve a country's standard of living in order to expand the clientele able to buy goods and services.

We do not expect an immediate acceptance and implementation of the policy of Common Development. We propose it for study as a concept that may influence real-world thinking at this historical point. Neither do we propose Common Development as the only means to eliminate the gradients between North and South. Even under the most optimistic assumptions, development will not be uniform around the world and rising standards of living will not soon erase the divides between poor and affluent. Differences *will* remain among nations as they have remained, to varying degrees, within well-functioning societies in the North. In some cases they will deepen, either temporarily or beyond the foreseeable horizon. We elaborate our calculus of what may be possible in the next chapter. What we do hope for from Common Development is a lessening of the asymmetries and the raising of the baseline standard of living of the largest fraction of the population of the Earth. We believe that combat flares when populations are under stress of basic wants, or feel systematically insecure. Such judgments were formed over years of the shortsightedness that characterized the great Cold War.

Our chief assumptions, then, are two. First, there is a broad, slowly shifting minimum level of well-being and security that leads most people to choose peaceful steps to further change. Second, the human race has now and can maintain the ability to provide that basic level to most people, even in the face of pressures for food, shelter, employment, and security emanating for the first time in history from the great postwar demographic transition that marks this century's end.

9

Improving the Quality of Life

The end goal of the complex process of Common Development is to improve the lives of the populations in the Second and Third Worlds while maintaining in the North some approximation of current overall levels, although familiar rates of economic growth are not expected to continue there over the century ahead.

What are the physical measures of what we collectively refer to as the "standard of living"? Cooked food, certainly, measured in calories consumed per day per person in a varying mix that offers adequate nutrients, is the most basic element of a population's standard of living. Clothing, shelter, and heating and the associated infrastructure, probably including running water and safe sewage disposal, come next, along with lighting and the telecommunications more and more prized today for entertainment, education, and community and nation building. The fraction of the available labor force gainfully employed is a key factor in the standard of living, as are levels of health and education, measured respectively by the life expectancy and infant mortality rates of a country's population, and the fraction who are able to enjoy easy and varied communications by image, text, and all the cultural arts. These are all roughly measurable but of course do not fully express the deepest needs of humankind. The term *quality of life* has come to stand for a wider goal, where both human relationships and the environment enter to enlarge the merely economic calculus.

Hope, the subjectively felt presence of opportunity for improving one's circumstances, once crudely measured by per capita income gain year after year, up to some level of material saturation, is an important factor in a nation's quality of life. It is this hope, neither too meagerly met nor too long deferred, that can buy the time the world needs. Its nurture in any country is probably the best diagnostic of the effectiveness of policy, both among those who have a high share of material goods and for those who remain by economic measures among the poor. Close attention from the United Nations and other actors in assessing public hope, both by competent sampling and by the more subtle means open to artists and writers, is of the highest value. Timely international help can sometimes revive lagging hopes, and we need it more and more.

Beginning with the Basics: Food

The U.N. Food and Agriculture Organization estimates—the result is far from true consensus—that about 20 percent of the global population, or somewhat more than a billion people, is currently chronically undernourished.[1] Increasing the food supply of many nations in the South must thus be a high priority of Common Development. But the problem today seems to be one of quality and distribution rather than gross food production. To feed a billion with a diet at the Chinese value—say one-quarter ton of grain per person per year—would requires 250 million tons of grain. But the undernourished are not without all grain; they are short by perhaps a third of what they need. Thus 100 million tons of grain would fill their bowls.

That is only about 5 percent of today's world production, and an eighth of all the cereals now fed to the livestock of the developed world. (Evenly distributed, the world's production of food grains would probably provide the world's current population with ample plant calories.) Though we now stand in sight of the long-sought end of hunger, it has not yet been attained, though both the relative and absolute numbers of undernourished have dropped slowly and steadily for a generation. The slowness of this process marks the refractory nature of so widely recognized a social ill, a phenomenon not unknown to city-dwelling Americans.

But the real issue is graver by far. The central problem is *not* the current sad undernourishment, nor can the solution lie mainly in the transfer of foodstuffs from food exporters like the United States, Canada, France, or Thailand (now the largest net exporter of rice). Those nations do not have enough grain. We know that men and women do not live by bread alone, but grains indeed do provide the staple starches that offer the bulk of human food energy. (Since crops vary yearly, our rounded values will fit some year of this decade; our attention is centered decades ahead, and a few years of mismatch do not affect broad conclusions.) The global cereal crop amounts in rounded total to 2 gigatons of grain per year (one gigaton is a billion tons).[2] The developing nations now produce more than half that total, about 1.2 gigatons. The developed ones provide the remaining 800 million tons, from which they feed their own quarter of the world's people on a diet that is much richer in fats, sweeteners, and animal products than the other three-quarters enjoy. The trade in grains entails mostly shipment of corn, much less of wheat, and tenfold less of rice. Rice is the largest of grain crops but it is eaten almost entirely in the same country where it grows,[3] much of it even by the poor families that grow it. (Big coastal cities form an exception.) The whole international trade in cereals amounts now to around 120 million tons a year of the global 2 gigatons grown.

The task ahead is less to feed the present 6 billion somewhat better, but to support in fifty years' time a much larger number, estimated to range between about 7.5 billion and as many as 12 billion persons (many of course children) after midcentury, when the great demographic change of the twentieth century will have more or less saturated. That surely means enough food in the developing world to feed not the present 4.5 billions but between 60 percent and 120 percent more of us sitting at the global table. That implies an increase in world grain crop of 0.7–1.4 gigatons.

The United States is by no means the largest grain producer, but it is the major exporter. U.S. cereal exports, now about three-quarters of all world grain exports, amount to 100 million tons, mostly in corn. The total American grain crop is about 320 million tons, of which half is used here and abroad as animal feed. In China and India together the cereal crops, largest in the world, are produced by the work of some 600 million people, nearly two-thirds of the labor force, in fields and paddies. The United States grows about half as much total grain annually but relies on the work of fewer than a million people on the grain lands. This hundredfold increase in labor productivity reflects the availability of ample, fertile rain-fed lands and of lengthy technical and educational investment in American agriculture. Notice that grain productivity *per acre* in China is now about the same as that for the United States. (Of course rice in warm lands may yield two or more crops per year.) It is the change from near-subsistence farming by households numbering in the hundred millions to industrialized agriculture, with at least a tenfold increase in labor productivity, that will allow these big countries to seek a high standard of living for their rural people too.

It is unlikely that North America could manage to send out even half the minimum increment of grain the developing nations need, a goal it could achieve only by ending its animal feeding while doubling its whole grain crop. And who would send the rest? Foreign trade and foreign aid in these staple crops can be seen as matters of opportunity or of extreme, usually transient, need. Perhaps the United States could export double or triple what it does now by reducing the two-thirds of the crop that it feeds to livestock (meat will be much dearer), and exploiting the accumulating gain in farm yield while the population at home stays nearly steady. But still a new gigaton each year can hardly come from the farms of the United States and the few smaller exporters.

The solution must lie mainly in the lands where the people and the land now are; they must continue largely *to do what they do now* and have always done—feed themselves, providing at least 80 percent or 90 percent of what they will need. Even the changes in habits and in prices that will one day demand cuts in the consumption of animal products (meats, dairy, poultry) worldwide will hardly meet the foreseen gap, roughly that gigaton of grain each year.

Farm products beyond the grains are of course important, but once major grain needs are met, it is likely that no major food wants will persist, even if transient shortages may demand for some people alternative foodstuffs once in a while. The ancient occupation of fishing is now showing strong signs of grave resource depletion,[4] at 100 million tons per year; but the yield from aquaculture is doubling every decade. Over the next few decades the fish farmers will take over from those who hunt the waters. They will achieve the required doubling or tripling of the catch, now about a third of the total food supply from animals.

Common Development efforts toward ensuring an adequate future food supply will have to concentrate on doubling the food grown in the developing world, mostly by efforts to increase the yield of the cultivated lands there. While the world's potentially arable land amounts to twice the area of what is sown today, most of the area is in Africa. Very little is in Asia, where populations will increase most vigorously in the next quarter-century. The gains there will have to come not only from increased know-how, as has been the case since the dawn of the Industrial Revolution in England, but from the introduction of new high-yield varieties of crops, from new skills and adaptation to the demands of crops and weather, and from some major new physical inputs. Those include power, equipment, and water sources for irrigation; more fertilizer and pesticides (or integrated pest control schemes now gaining use); well-chosen agricultural machinery, often usable at small scale; improved storage and transport of harvested crops; and simple field instrumentation and control and better weather prediction, to guide farmers in managing their crops. More and better-spread agronomic advice, now broadly available in the developed nations, and with it the spread of the best local practices, will add substantially to the yields of lands already under cultivation.

The present system is headed by a dozen specialized international agricultural research centers—the fomenters of the Green Revolution and its successors.[5] They have done a great deal to improve the food supply of the poorer world regions with a modest investment, now totaling only $300 million each year. The rise of biotechnology almost ensures a big increase, much of it of course to be paid both by successful farmers and by the satisfied consumers. Technology and know-how will remain the major contributions Common Development can make to the globe's food production. The World Bank has estimated the world cost of the increased technical support to be about $30 billion a year, triple the sum spent in 1985.

Education of farm families, new price policies to improve farmers' lot, and capital spent to enrich the amenities of rural life will be the tasks of the developing homelands. The incentive for such actions is strong indeed, and it does not seem unlikely that the incremental growth in average yield on the acreage that has been responsible for four-fifths of the overall crop increment since 1900[6] will continue. The world grain crop has tripled quite uniformly during the last four decades. A doubling of the world crop appears quite feasible by next midcentury, though under close attention by all the nations.

One-fifth of the increase since 1900 has come from newly cultivated areas. That growth can continue both in the Americas and in Africa even though it has long stopped in Europe and slowed to very little in Asia, but it will go on; Africa is now the continent with the fastest projected increase in demand for foodstuffs, but also boasts the largest supply of arable yet unused land. There the constraints of water and soil remain; protecting the present irrigated lands and preventing soil erosion clearly will require investment of both capital and much local labor. Indeed, the well-demonstrated ability of market forces to keep food away from those whose needs are not supported by income here presents an opportunity. Cash payments to local near-subsistence farmers for their labor in off-seasons to improve the soil and water management infrastructure of their land is a happy way to meet both their immediate needs and future prospects—this is a long-run antifamine policy. International support will be drawn upon here.

Energy

The fundamental physical quantity with which the material support of life in any nation most closely correlates is the energy available per capita. A primary focus of Common Development will have to entail providing the requisite amounts of appropriate energy-generating capacity to developing and underdeveloped nations.

Here we need some familiar measure of energy use. Americans buy electrical energy by the kilowatt-hour, at an average retail cost of some eight cents delivered.[7] But we use so many kilowatt-hours each year that the meaning is not easy to grasp. Moreover, the power company uses much more energy in generating each kilowatt-hour than the consumer receives; the energy costs in coal or other fuel (the so-called primary energy) are about three times the delivered useful amount. With present technology the wasted two-thirds are mostly thrown up the stacks or into the cooling water in the form of heat. Most of us buy the energy to run our cars by the gallon of gas, not by the kilowatt-hour, but once again lost engine heat takes two-thirds of the energy content of the gasoline. Much other energy is directly used as heat, which also can be measured its an equivalent steady flow of kilowatts.

The figures for overall power use we present below do not refer to actual electric power only. They denote the equivalent in power of all the flow of energy delivered to users in forms that include gasoline, coal, and the rest. Many people still depend on "traditional" fuels—firewood and brush, crop and stubble wastes, cattle droppings, and other sources; these share the property of having their origins in recent sunlight. "Commercial" fuels—coal, oil, natural gas—represent the huge inventory of stored sunlight from the geological past.

Table 9.1 will bring energy closer to experience. That is useful since we need to understand aggregate power needs (such as the rate of energy flow) over billions of users and yet keep some feeling for what the individual experience is.

A flow of 1 terawatt (a trillion watts) can be maintained for one year by burning about 1 gigaton (or 1 billion metric tons) of standard soft coal. The great stream of oil that flows by pipeline and by tanker out of the lands around the Persian Gulf amounts to a steady energy flow of about 1.5 terawatts. Just what is the needed amount and the appropriate form of power generation depends on a wide context. An industrializing country like Mexico has totally different energy needs and priorities than a country that remains rural, such as Niger or Morocco.

The long-remarked correlation between a nation's gross domestic product per capita and its primary energy consumption per capita runs as high as 80 to 90 percent.[8] This is partly an artifact of history. Energy use per dollar of income has declined sharply in this century; efficiency has made a strong difference. Nor does higher energy use in itself bring an ever-better standard of living. The main new result is that quality of life levels off even as energy use increases beyond a given value. Recent studies that use levels of health and education in addition to income to judge quality of life show

Table 9.1
Examples of energy use (expressed as a steady flow at the source)

	Rate of energy flow (power)
Ordinary fluorescent lamp	100 W (watts)
Large color TV	1,000 W (= 1 kilowatt)
Big highway diesel truck	1,000,000 W (= 1 megawatt)
Modern big-city electrical power plant	3,000,000,000 W (= 3 gigawatt)
Entire U.S. electrical power supply	750,000,000,000 W (= 0.75 terawatt)

Source: Vaclav Smil, *General Energetics* (New York: Wiley, 1991).

that the strong correlation between energy use and standard of living saturates at about 70 gigajoules (16 million calories) of energy per capita annually, or 2.0 kilowatts per capita of commercial heat and power (see figure 9.1). Vaclav Smil finds dramatic improvement in infant mortality, literacy, life expectancy, and university attendance as energy consumption grows, all saturating at about 2 kilowatts per person.[9] There the steep curve of growth reaches a sharp knee at an overall standard of living comparable to that of France in the 1960s.[10] In that time and place most households possessed good stoves, refrigerators, bathrooms, washing machines, and central heating. Much beyond that and saturation appears (see figure 9.2).

What that meant in everyday life is neither unfamiliar nor extreme: nourishing and varied food every day (much of it cooked), safe water for drinking and sanitation, inexpensive clothing in some variety, comfortable shelter with light and heat (perhaps cooling in hot climates), some furniture

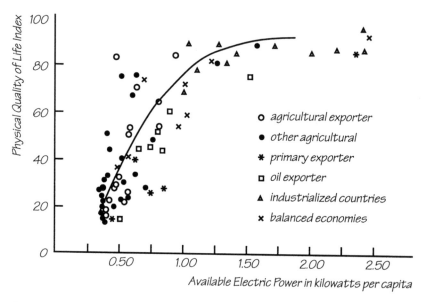

Figure 9.1
Correlation of the quality of life with the amount of electric power available. Increased energy availability improves the overall quality of life independently of the dominant economic activity of the society, but up to a point (1.5–2 kilowatts/person), beyond which the quality of life hardly changes with additional available power. *Note:* Each available kilowatt of electricity requires for its production about three kilowatts of primary power in the form of fuel.

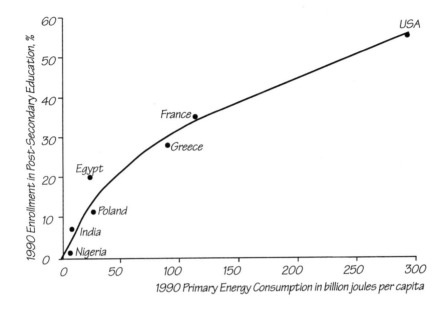

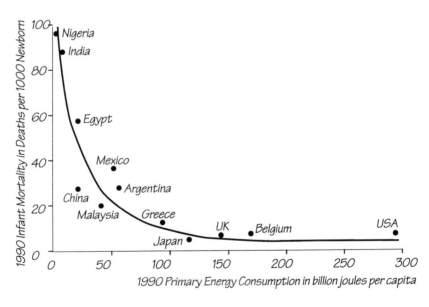

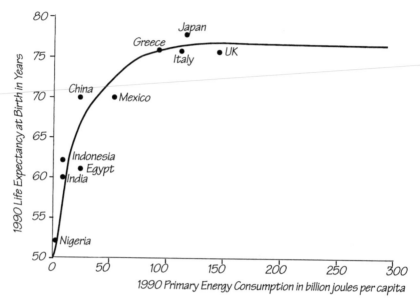

Figure 9.2 (Previous page, top and bottom; and above)
Improvement in the levels of university education, infant mortality, and life expectancy, with primary energy consumption in various nations during 1990. The benefits of additional primary energy appear to saturate at about 150 billion joules per person per year, or about five kilowatts per capita.

and household goods, widespread public health measures (including immunization and medical care, especially in time of urgency), literacy and the chance for higher education, communication, news, and entertainment, and increasing personal mobility by auto. Of course the estimated energy flow includes not only that used on the spot but also the energy spent to create and run the industrial and public services that produce the needed goods.

We take 2 kilowatts per person as a basic measure of what Common Development has to achieve for the total energy sector. The amount of energy input needed to achieve this standard of living, however, can be cut almost by half once we realize that *end-uses of energy are now more efficient than in the 1960s.* These efficiencies are already widely available in the industrialized world. This brings the goal for Common Development closer: increase the energy flow some 0.3 to 0.7 kilowatt per person for the 80 percent of the global population in the Second and Third Worlds, to be achieved within the next twenty-five or thirty years. In underdeveloped nations this will require outright financial aid and technical assistance. In the more industrialized nations of the South, the need will be for cheap capital to borrow and for favorable treatment of their industrial products in the markets of the North, so that they may earn the funds to purchase the commercial energy supplies and the capital plant they need (oil, natural gas, coal, and uranium, and modern plant for energy generation and end-use conversion).

Fast Growers and Villagers

To form a realistic estimate of the overall cost of economic growth in the South (in fact only Brazil and a couple of its neighbors, Java, and southern Africa hold sizable growing populations south of the equator), we divided the world's peoples into three groups. These groupings—our frontispiece map supports the result nicely—are based not on nations but on present common economic bases and expected rates of growth. This led us to surprising results that conventional categories seem to obscure.

We find three clearly distinct categories of people. The first are the residents of the developed world, areas that are very productive and technically advanced and where only a few percent of the population still lives on or near the land. The capital on hand for industry and services is enormous. These economies are mature, and rather predictable. They include about one-fifth of the world's people.

The second category is the fast-growing countries, where industry is well in place but the farm population is still an important fraction of the people, although not the majority. In these states the population is no longer growing rapidly, and in exceptional China, the most populous of all, the head count is nearing a plateau.

Third is a large and still growing group of people, some 2 billion, who still live by subsistence farming, with low inputs and outputs not much beyond their own needs. Their presence on the farm is a current necessity, for there seems no quick way to provide enough capital to move them off the paddy or the little field and yet retain the crops they live by. Modernization will not fully reach them during the first half of the century to come. We call them the "villagers," for they dwell mainly in a million villages all across East and South and Southeast Asia, and in the rural settlements of South America and Africa (see table 9.2).

"Traditional" fuels, mostly locally produced, are vital to these people.[11] Overall they form a floor to energy use by poor rural people that amounts to a few hundred watts per capita worldwide. The shortage of fuelwood, for instance, has long been a grievance as population increase has fed demand, met mainly by long laborious effort by rural women. Villagers count on some such sources for essential light, cooking, and seasonal heating. But in many places even that minimal resource is coming to be seen as insufficient.

The earliest goal for energy use by midcentury is therefore modest: can the world provide 1.5 kilowatts per person or a little more for most of the global population? Those left out will mostly include the poor farmers of staple crops who continue to use traditional nonmechanized means. They are the world's "villagers."

The product of their labor is staple grain, still indispensable. They will require hope, at least the basics: a near-end to seasonal chronic malnutrition and genuinely eased access to water and household fuel, and some share in the new amenities. Modest amounts of local power from wind, solar stoves, photovoltaics, or some other source less capital intensive than far-flung power lines and big turbines in central power generation stations, can bring valuable benefits from the industrial world, like adequate lights and cooking fuel, on to TV, telecommunications, even refrigeration. Cellular phones promise real benefits to most villagers for low investment; one to a few such phones per village would go a long way toward slowly ending isolation.

The needed increase of new energy per head ought to be achieved without long delay. World population will grow by about 3.2 billion between 1995 and 2025 or 2030.[12] Half of that rise will occur within a dozen of

Table 9.2
Population (in billions) according to economic activity

	1950	1995	2030	2060
World	2.5	5.4	8.5	11
Mature economies	1.1	1.1	1.4	1.5
Fast-growing economies		1.5	2.4	5
"Villagers" economies	1.4	2.7	4.7	4.5

the largest developing nations. The economically fast-growing countries among them will see an increase of a billion or so, and the "villagers" will gain nearly 2 billion, to reach a 4.7 billion head count. Given their present commercial energy consumption, it will be necessary to raise the energy flow to fast growers by 3 terawatts a generation ahead. Another 2 terawatts will be needed to double the energy available per capita to the villagers.

We undertake to sketch what the world might look like as a whole by 2030, even more sketchily by midcentury, and to calculate the approximate required capital investment and aid in the context of Common Development that could achieve the anticipated growth. We also calculate how much of the funding would have to come from the North and by when. We cannot simply extrapolate from the past, because the power and fuel costs grow to become a major portion of the developing economies. Avoiding the cost of large-scale increases of power generation capacity by focusing on end-use efficiency seems unpromising: it requires abandoning much functioning equipment.

The demographic transition is only now beginning among the "villagers." These inhabitants are the ones who will have to provide the largest portion of the extra gigaton of grains each year to staunch their own hunger, among the 7 billion who will inhabit the Second and Third Worlds by 2030. By then, the *villagers'* standard of living must improve if they are to stay at their appointed task of growing the doubled crops the increased population needs. While the productivity per acre of land they till is high, their individual labor productivity is low. They will need added energy in the form of water-pumping power, fertilizers, and fuel for some agricultural machinery. The amount of energy needed will vary from place to place. India, for instance, has irrigation power that now reaches a third of its village population.

Here we set forth our forecasts as a roughly reasonable model of what might happen. We label the three categories: *mature economies, fast-growth economies*, and the *villagers*. The mature include North America, Europe, the Russian Federation, Japan, and a few other well-off countries. The fast-growth places include China and part of India, some of Southeast Asia, other South Asian countries, and the more urbanized areas of South America and Africa. The villagers are found in all of the rural lands outside what we called the mature economies, many raising crops of rice, corn, wheat, cassava, millet, and sorghum, and some with livestock.

Much of the 2 terawatts needed to double the energy flow rate to the *villagers* (see table 9.3) over the next thirty years will be in the form of small (5–50 kilowatts) local sources of electrical power such as photovoltaic arrays or new high-tech windmills. These technologies now cost from $500–1,000 per kilowatt installed, so the total cost per terawatt will be about half a trillion to a trillion dollars over the next generation—no more than $30 billion per year during that time. More centrally produced power is often quoted as costing about the same—$1,000 per kilowatt.

So to a rough approximation, the 5 terawatt we project will be needed outside the industrialized North will cost $150 billion a year, the figure the World Bank quotes as the cost of bringing the developing world up to the benchmark of 2 kilowatts per person and improving the standard of living of most of the globe's villagers.

In table 9.3, we allow some decrease in energy use by the developed world in the next generation owing to the benefits of higher efficiency and price-induced frugality. We anticipate that another billion people will reach the 2-kilowatt-per-person benchmark, but that villagers will see only a modest rise, since their number will almost double and their current consumption level is almost ten times below our goal of 2 kilowatts.

The Costs of Common Development

We can now reach for an overall estimate of the total cost of the policy of Common Development for the next thirty years or so. The World Bank's estimate of about $30 billion a year for technical support of the production

Table 9.3
Energy needs (totals are in terawatts, and kWpc = kilowatts per capita)

	1950 Total	1950 kWpc	1995 Total	1995 kWpc	2030 Total	2030 kWpc	2060 Total	2060 kWpc
World	1.5	.6	12	2	20	2.3	26	2.3
Mature economies			9	8.2	11	7.8	8	5
Fast-growing economies			2	1.3	5+	2	12	2.4
Villagers			1	.3	3+	.6	6	1.3

Source: *Handbook of International Trade and Development Statistics*, United Nations, 1992.

of food worldwide will total nearly a trillion dollars by 2025. Implementing our proposals for improving energy flow to fast growers and villagers will require another $5 trillion.

Improving the rate of enrollment in primary and secondary schools in the developing world to match the levels of the industrialized countries is inexpensive: that will cost about $5 billion a year. Another $18 billion per annum will be needed to improve children's health and to reduce the infant mortality rate worldwide, according to a 1990 UNICEF report. To counterbalance the demographic pressures that the reduction in infant mortality will cause, Common Development policy would have to also address birthrates in many Second and Third World nations. Financing a 20 percent increase in use of contraception worldwide would cost about $7 billion, according to a study by the Congressional Budget Office.[13] This amounts to a final trillion over the next 30 years. In toto, then, $7 trillion will have to be devoted to the task of lessening the steep asymmetries between North and South over the next thirty years—or an average of some $230 billion per year. At the start, a large fraction will have to come from the strongly capitalized North in the form of loans, investments, and outright aid. But as the fast-growing regions of the world reach the mid-twentieth-century standard of Western Europe, less and less input will be required from the developed world.

Many industrial activities we now see restricted to the West, Russia, and Japan will become open to China, and to others soon thereafter. Steel to software, chemicals to biotechnology, even new technical developments for consumers and producers alike will begin to come from the newer economies, whose powers will be broadly comparable to those of today's North, albeit much smaller in breadth and depth of production and of innovation. The newly developed countries will become leaders or serious contenders in many niches of industry and modern services. GE, Phillips, Hitachi, Mercedes-Benz will be joined in everyday speech by new names and new ideas from China, India, Brazil, Indonesia, and more in a few decades. What Japan could do the others will soon do at the same scale, always against a wider background.

These new powers, bulging with young people, able to draw upon impressive new industries, will always have warlike options. It is plain that the alternative paths we propose, Common Security and Common

Development, become more and more attractive to the well-to-do, and need be kept a visibly wise policy for the receptor states as well. Clearly a one-sided offer of outside aid to such a new group of powerful states will become harder to justify; the hope will be to induce these newer entrants to provide some help to states and regions—the villagers—still behind. Even the developed lands have plenty of wants.

In early 1997 Deng Xiaoping, last of the dominating heroes of Mao's Long March, died at 92. His long time spent offstage seems to have eased the succession to national leadership in China, where the marketplace has grown to somewhat greater economic weight than the total of the state-run enterprises there. The country is clearly a mixed economy, moreover one without substantial democracy. Our remarks on feedback apply: the market has worked wonders in stimulating both industry and agriculture, with rapid increases in GNP. Foreign investment in China has helped produce an extensive export industry. China may enjoy more than a third of all private investment in the developing world. The total annual flow of private capital, main mark of the global economy, to developing countries is now some $250 billion. This is about what we feel is needed to help world Common Development, and as much as four to six times the total aid flow.

We did not foresee so rapid a change in Chinese policy. But we would expect that the market's swift amplification of successful growth and its counterpart, social and economic neglect of places where profit is not favored, will step by step lead to change again. Already the Chinese economy has begun to put aside the villagers of the interior and set many farmers adrift from the land, without any social safety net save growth. Exactly these events show the limitations of marketplace feedback, exacerbated by the presence of a strong but undemocratic state. The familiar flowering of unreasoned elements of popular life, such as consumer excess, public gambling, widening corruption, and interest in the occult is plain.

A mixed economy, capital and consumer markets generally tempered by regulation, taxation, resource limits, price rises, and popular will, is slowly on its way. That is the more likely scenario because the path of growth, indispensable to market success, cannot continue unguided into the long run. We believe that China will follow current developments for another couple of decades as we have outlined them, though not without the shortcomings described. We Americans will not watch in calm detachment for too long. We have our own visible if little-heeded pitfalls, though for us democratic feedback remedies lie closer at hand than they do yet in China.

In the last couple of years since the change in China's leadership, a number of hints, so far mainly anecdotal, strengthen our view that overly simple models of economic life will not prove permanent in the face of change. The movement of people from inland villages to build and fill the new factories of coastal China has continued, if slowly. But some lively people flow back too, to bring inland the new ideas—truck repair, farm services, health work—they learned in travel. The village elections now nationwide in China, while by no means fully democratic, are all the same a serious novelty seen at work in many places. The recent Peoples' Congress of early 1998 heard the leaders call for a huge investment of funds for improving the roads, bridges, public buildings, desperately neglected pollution controls, water supplies, sewage treatment, and the like—an outsized Works Progress Administration to ease the harsh unemployment that will accompany the coming cut in unprofitable state enterprise and its rusted iron rice bowl. Is this not the shadowy hand of Lord Keynes glimpsed within an economy that has clung to its own mix of Marx, Mao, and Adam Smith?

10

The Limits of the Practical

So far we have outlined a coherent set of proposals toward a more peaceful world—one probable path, far from certain, toward security for the United States in a stable world late in the next century. Our country will not, because it cannot, live in fortified isolation; our scheme for U.S. security therefore encompasses the entire globe. Anything more parochial would fly in the face of objective realities: the disasters of regional war, the inexorable results of the demographic transition now at hand, and the pervasive character of slowly spreading threats to the global environment. The changes in mobile air and water are by now global, and our understanding and concern must grasp that expansion.

In the previous chapter we examined what Common Development might mean, with clear emphasis on the next three decades with their slowing growth in population. Here we try to describe, in hazy outline, what we anticipate the world might be like even fifty or sixty years beyond that, as other limits appear within the broad community of nations, both among the billion people of the now-industrialized North and the 8 billion or more, the huge majority, in the now-developing lands. The uncertainties of the future are wide, but they become less significant as we examine concretely, if only briefly, what we can already recognize in the world of a near-doubled humanity ahead. We sketch an approach to the varied limits that circumstances fix.

Nations and Their People

A bare majority of all the people of Earth live in the six most populous nations.[1] In order of size, they are China, India, the United States, Indonesia, Brazil, and Russia. (China and India together hold more than a third of all human heads.) A working majority would include the four countries next in population: a stable Japan and three fast-growing lands: Pakistan, Bangladesh, and Nigeria. (Each of those three houses above three-fourths of the current population of the Russian Federation.)

If we add together the people within all the nations whose populations outnumber the 30 million in our most populous state, California, the list includes some 25 sizable countries, closing with Argentina, and more than 80 percent of all humans. To include every country with a population as large as Ohio's we would need to add 35 more, the largest Canada, with Portugal, Greece, and Honduras at the end of the list. By now our list of 70 nations, all with populations above 10 million, would include 95 percent of humanity.

The count of smaller member nations runs on to about 90 more, to total about 160 legal national entities. There are still more, about 50 nationlike groups as well, many of them more populous than the smallest U.N. members. Mainly they are island dwellers, physically separated from the nations upon which they are legally dependent. The largest of these 50 in population is American Puerto Rico. All these places form the theater for discussions of war and peace, of life and death, through this twentieth century and most of the next, crystallized as it is mainly around nation-states.

A few special categories within the population deserve special notice: the world's active military personnel, about 25 million under arms; the world's refugees, now about 20 or 25 million as well; and the women of the world, an electoral majority of about 53 percent, though one badly underserved by both economies and states and generally underrepresented in policymaking at every level. A related feature of the species worldwide is its age distribution. The developing lands, where the percentages of both births and deaths per year are high, of course have the largest fraction of children under 15: they amount to 45 percent of all Africans, 20 percent of Europeans, and 20 percent of residents of the United States.

We must not neglect the organizations of civil society worldwide that are not states; many are present in the halls of the United Nations as nongovernmental organizations (NGOs) and exert fast-growing influence, often weighing in as important early advocates of essential change. States are certainly not the only actors, although they provide the formal structure for most of the topics we consider; indeed, sometimes they are even the adversaries of large groups of their own citizens. The very number and diversity of NGOs forces them offstage for our study, though they are never in fact absent.

An Urban World

During the demographic transition, cities will grow. The 70 percent urbanization of the richer countries is not likely to spread worldwide, but the 30 percent of city dwellers we count now in the poorer countries will probably grow beyond 50 percent. Urbanization increases much more rapidly today as waves of poor people flood cities from farmlands in China, South Asia, and Africa. In the big cities the newcomers dwell all too often in squalor and societal neglect, sometimes as a harsh surprise, sometimes as a hard bargain they accept, hoping to put behind themselves for good the steady drudgery, the monotonous surroundings, and the stagnation of village life spent cultivating croplands less favored by nature and human decision. Often opportunity, however thin and deferred, is seen as the city's gift, particularly for the children of overworked village women.

Almost everywhere cities grow apace, chiefly through migration from the rural world. A recent list of megacities—metropolitan centers whose population in A.D. 2000 is estimated to be more than the 10 million of Ohio—includes twenty-one.[2] The largest of all is Tokyo (at 26 million), followed in size by São Paulo, Bombay, Shanghai, and New York. The other sixteen proceed from Mexico City to Cairo. Not one of them is in Europe!

These big cities will multiply in number as well. The two dozen megacities of the year 2000 will become 40 or 50 by midcentury, most of them in Africa and Asia. Big cities, not the giants but those with more than 1 million but fewer than 10 million people, now a list of 300 or 400, will multiply to above 1,000, again most of them new names to all but the well traveled: for one example in each continent, recall Abidjan, Fortaleza, Hermosilla, Kuala Lumpur, Perth.

Their people will mostly work in factories and offices; city life will continue as the dynamo of economic life. Improvement of the lot of most city dwellers will become the norm. That is not to say that new villagers coming to the cities will escape the hardships of the South Bronx or even of the steep hillsides of Rio. The marginal itinerant workers and ragpickers of today will not vanish, but the increase in their numbers will slow. The benefits of official and private investment will come to favor the villagers more than it does today if their crops are to provide a share of the needed food, though they will still see a relatively low income and living standard. The states will slowly raise the barriers to free migration as well as find new inducements for people to stay in slowly improving villages, close to their precious fields, if not bountiful at least sunlit in an epoch of food scarcity.

Profound economic differences, though not so much the cultural ones that part the world, will begin to fade both in the regions around the great cities and in the well-served and more productive rural lands. Even now such change is visible. The deeper variety inherent in human life is hardly in danger; though languages and cultures surely interact and shift as they accommodate newly commonplace flu shots, television, home refrigerators, and banks, they are by no means becoming homogenized. The growing elderly populations of the North as well as the increasingly youthful majorities of the South guarantee a zesty, unpredictable mix of interests and traditions. Content still matters. We will not live by cola alone.

Nor will world culture itself lag; all the arts and sciences, old and new, the high and the popular, will flow out of these newly empowered and populous lands whenever circumstances favor. What is coming is not at all any sort of an end to human history, but rather the first opportunity for humanity to perform on a stage that is truly global.

Telecommunications

Since the adoption in 1948 of the U.S. policy of coercive security, or containment of communism mostly by military effort, drastic changes have occurred in how peoples around the world organize their governance and form their political beliefs. Technology has placed in the hands of all who would shape national policy a new tool, potent in the shorter run and of uncertain long-run impact: television. Vivid visual experience is now instantaneously transmitted from almost any point of the world and inexpensively received worldwide with a billion households potentially attentive. Video cameras and recorders, even satellite uplinks, are no rarities nowadays, and their widespread presence makes possible worldwide viewing even of some events unrecorded by official media, as the Los Angeles Police Department can document.

The resulting creation of widespread new perceptions linked to very old roots renders television a powerful new factor in world affairs. Its ubiquitous presence matches the global proportions of the challenges humanity faces: nuclear danger, regional wars and disorder, the demographic transition and its effects, and gross environmental deterioration. By using the geosynchronous orbit above the equator—a most precious world resource—to transmit its images, now augmented by the use of multiple satellites in closer orbits, global television easily crosses national borders. Its images tend to erode the concept and practice of the sovereign nation-state, alone behind its inviolate frontiers, their penetration constituting a cause of war, for it is protection from physical aggression that has long been the raison d'être of national military establishments. Words from afar have long carried messages affecting public order, but images may enter more deeply still. Famine and earthquake have moved many millions from afar, and political events as well. That tank challenged by an unarmed young man near Tianenmen Square remains memorable, and the bodies the world saw daily floating out of Rwanda down the Kigera River by tens of thousands conveyed an unmatched shock during the summer of 1994. It is true that indifference can grow out of repetition even to so terrible a stimulus, but major political consequences are probable. States can limit both what is sent from their territories and what their own people can watch, but it is no easy matter. Sometimes the broadcast will be welcomed: world coverage of a nuclear or biological attack would be a powerful deterrent to an attacker and a persuasive appeal by the victim. This emotional linkage of the wide world is an important new determinant of world opinion, here to stay and growing in influence.

Another major effect of the new telecommunications is a truly tidal flow of transactions in the world markets. These are often managed automatically by prepared computer programs fed with the newest quotations. The result has been an enormous new fluidity in all arbitrage and broadly in the transfer of capital funds. One reliable figure can be cited. The most complex options of modern security markets—the derivatives—are so handled. Total annual trade in that single specialized sector of investment (or speculation?) amounts to four or five times the entire GDP of the largest economy, the United States. The markets as a whole are at least an order of magnitude larger.

The structure thus built—it rises much beyond mere transaction reports—is a part of today's amazing capital fluidity, on which the transnational corporate economy is largely based. Funds flow very much more freely than can real goods and more complex services. It appears that capital transfer has all but escaped its limitations. Like any enduring free ride, this one, too, profitable in the short run, is unaware of its own externalities. The feedback loop is open, or at least very weak. This seems a serious latent instability of the global corporate system, parallel to the ruin of the centrally planned economies of the old Soviet bloc.

A major revision would appear to be in order, bringing the markets themselves and corporations globally under much increased regulation and national and even international taxation. Those who are not shareholders but who remain affected claim attention: employees, customers, suppliers of both specific inputs and the wider infrastructure, those who live downstream from production effluents—a status that in itself is turning global—and even investors in alternatives. The claims of all these interests are most likely to be met politically via the nation-states; see the American newspapers of 1996 for widespread comment after the stock market crash.

Automobiles: A Second Species

The auto is so salient a feature of today's richer economies, so thirsty for its fuel, so urgent a competitor for clean air and wide open space, that a look at its future among the new billions of people is natural. Nowadays we soft-shelled humans share the thronged earth with our hard-shelled symbiots on wheels, the automobile species. Today's automass well outweighs human biomass, maybe even doubles it.[3] The hood count now runs about a tenth of our own human head count. The largest of all manufacturing industries, the world auto industry, now hatches about a million new cars every week.

But those autos are most unevenly spread. In the United States there is one car or truck for every 1.4 persons: more than enough seats to give

Americans and their baggage a national lift all at once. China, by no means the least motorized of lands, has instead almost 1,500 people for each motor vehicle. Surely that ratio is in for change.

It is a surprise to see straight-line growth since 1960 in the U.S. auto census. A pause in the last three or four years is the main variation to be seen. In Europe the creatures now multiply pretty steadily as well. The fuel use of passenger cars will rather surely be cut by a factor of two, perhaps even three, mostly through lighter vehicles made of new materials and optimized flow both of intake and exhaust gases. Trucks will, as now, be many fewer than cars but consume about the same total amount of fuel. Trucks and buses, heavy and light, haul over medium distances and long hours most food, fuel, goods, and people. They seem likely to increase in number in rough proportion to the world economic output. All vehicles will multiply more slowly than in the past as they crowd their own roads, and the external costs of keeping them both at rest and in motion will rise.

By another measure, though, their fecundity is much more in doubt. We look for the world's personal autos to multiply less rapidly than global power use; if the new designs operate at half the fuel cost, those new cars will consume under 1 terawatt of energy equivalent by 2050, and the harder-working trucks will use about 1 terawatt more—a total energy use hardly more than today but within a much larger future economy. The gift of personal mobility plainly still infatuates us, especially in North America, its newer cities largely built around the auto. In the United States about 90 percent of the work force rides to work daily in car, van, or truck; public transport, walking, or working at home make up the other tithe. Japan and Europe, although less motorized, signal that the attraction Americans feel is common.

In any case the bill that this engine species will present for our personal mobility, while high, is not yet intolerable. The auto's tenth of total world projected power use midcentury is likely to be an overestimate; but complete support for all those cars ahead will prove demanding. It will be a long time before the networks of vehicle roads accessible to the numerous villagers are as dense as those of Iowa.

It may be that the present densely populated Netherlands—with no auto industry but with well-managed railroads, streetcars, taxis, and plenty of bicycles—suggests that a modern economy can be somewhat unhooked from autos. Indeed, world auto use gradients will no doubt smooth out. If the Chinese double their auto manufacturing capacity each decade—as they now propose to do—they might in thirty or forty years gain the plant and labor to build 10 million new cars per year. That would roughly match today's leading producers, the United States and Japan, but it would add only a modest 20 percent to present world production of motor vehicles.

All the main personal gains that development offers come to working households quite readily at 1.5 kilowatts of power per capita given updated efficiencies, save perhaps the one we here focus on: that long-distance personal mobility that is the coveted gift of the private automobile. When the French reached the equivalent power level in the 1960s, they drove one car for every eight or ten citizens; this appears to us a plausible forecast worldwide for those who will reach that modest level of consumption, where the gains in quality of life accruing from increased energy consumption begin to level off.

It is a good bet that a billion private cars will be driving the world's roads by 2050, though disproportionately fewer near the lagging villages. At steady state that world would produce almost double the present number of cars, 100 million a year, but it is both likely and urgent that they be lighter, cheaper, and much less fuel thirsty. Extension of auto use to most village families will await the emergence of new power sources later in the century or may never come, as other personal goals become more attractive.

Food, Water, and Soil

The food needs of the more populous world of midcentury are by no means easy to foresee accurately. The usual rules of thumb are hardly good enough; variations in people's age, size, and climate of residence make real differences of as much as a quarter or a third of the roughly calculable amounts. A factor of two increase in food output has already been on the books for almost a century; we can likely do it again. Even the more cautious forecasters seem to grant that.

Certainly the constraints of water and soil remain. Some effort at avoiding salination of long-irrigated lands, and at reducing the erosion of fertile soil on rain-fed farms, clearly will require considerable investment of outside capital and much local labor. Severe drought, monsoon failure, and the rest are like El Niño events of history.

We need a larger food reserve in the productive Americas as world population grows worldwide; we need all the organizational and technical help we can get. But once more we come away with a reasoned view. Taking bad with good even when not expecting a forever-smiling future, we can manage a modest steady improvement for billions, though not soon for all.

Plant breeding by novel forms of gene exchange is sure to grow in importance. This is a powerful tool only recently made available. Even the supply of nitrogen directly from the air suggests possible legumelike modifications in the staple grains. Major changes in the harvest index—how much crop biomass resides in the edible portions of plants—is also likely. Tissue and microbial culture is now a reality for certain small-scale production of certain drugs and flavorings. These techniques might eventually imply changes in agriculture not matched in 10,000 years: major crop growth within sealed plastic containers, so that sunlight could be used in any not-too-cold climate, with greatly reduced need for water and for soil nutrients. Such dreams cannot become reality at large scale by 2050, but might they not arrive by 2100?

Whence the Energy?

World energy supply stands in a strange position. For the long run it waits upon a decline in consumer demand, a population decrease, or fundamental technological change, all three plausible, practical, but surely long-delayed outcomes. The distant goal of energy "sustainability"—however it is interpreted—may be reached in a century or so without any dominating environmental risk. But for the next five decades we have no such surety. This is the time of the global transition. Surely it can come as no surprise that it is the chanciest time of all.

The rapid growth of the oil supply seen when the Middle Eastern fields first came into large production at the close of World War II will almost surely not be repeated. Crises concerning the price and availability of oil may very well return. But widely usable oil and gas will not disappear in the next thirty or even sixty years. Reserves of oil and gas are famously slippery to estimate, although solid coal is easier to measure. Conventional estimates of hydrocarbon reserves forecast about 2,000 gigatons still to come, equivalent to a constant energy flow of some 10 terawatts for some centuries. Uranium reserves might come to outproduce all the hydrocarbons by a few fold, if we take the most optimistic view of the use of fission technology ahead. That option seems likely to reopen in a few decades; right now the trend is strongly against more use of fission, and it cannot be counted on soon.

Large-scale hydropower promises less, no more than a few long-lasting terawatts, and only after sedulous effort, high investment, and political struggle over the major externalities. Large hydro is a relatively reliable technology for a time scale of a century or so. But it is highly site-specific, and not all attractive projects will prove to be worth the expensive candle.

Solar electric power from photovoltaic installations is likewise unlimited by fuel, by greenhouse gas wastes, or by the needed materials, mainly sand. Like farming, it demands a broad sunlit area. The power needed by villagers for improved quality of life—what we see as a beginning step to 1.5 kilowatt per village head—would require a generating area per person of some 50 square meters covered by photovoltaic film, allowing some space for auxiliary needs, access spaces, and so on. The lands that these same farmers tend span upward from a practical minimum of 1,000 square meters of land per person. Providing this solar electric power source seems quite possible within that basic limit of area, given an optimistic estimate of technical availability and capital cost. But the sun shines only by day; either some additional energy storage on site or some expensive or novel transmission system from afar is required to provide any power at all after dark. As a complement to daytime solar electric power, needed energy might be transported worldwide by ship or by pipeline, as liquid natural methane or crude oil are shipped now.

Economical use of photovoltaic technology is hopeful if not yet firm. The first photovoltaic plant of good-sized capacity, its 150 megawatts reaching only a tenth to a fifth of the power rating for large fossil-fueled power plants, is now under construction in the Southern California desert, scheduled to feed its power output into the state electric power grid.

But the billion rural villagers are much harder to serve, since no flexible means of energy storage is yet cheap at small scale. Villagers, like everyone else, will want to watch TV or read, to cook, and to seek some extra heat while the sun is down; that requires inexpensive low-maintenance energy storage, for which present technology offers little. Storage batteries are most frequently used, but their inadequacy is well known. Using PV or wind to pump water is fine when the water is close to the end use sought—household, livestock, or garden—but converting excess power into household electricity for use at night is not cheap. Windmills share that need for storage of electricity, and they too are site-specific.

Photovoltaic costs for localized village sources will be fixed by the technology's durability under rural conditions—dust, dirt, locusts, hailstorms—and by the cost of nighttime energy storage. Perhaps some of the solar-fed systems might be arranged to produce a portable fuel such as methanol, or even the minimally polluting gaseous hydrogen (contained under pressure or absorbed in reusable metal sponge), using as steady inputs only air, water, and sunny lands. That fuel could then be burned at leisure in transport vehicles, in households, or even in industries near the sun-collecting area. It is not clear that we can gain even the modest amount of energy we forecast from local use of sunshine without a power grid, though there is ample room for hope, the more since initial village uses of power are apt to be the cheaper ones such as lights, TV, perhaps wireless (cellular) telephone services. This form of power is marginal for cooking. House heating and cooling, irrigation pumping, crop processing, and supplying running water and other motorized aids to daily labor will largely be deferred until more power becomes inexpensively practical, local or not.

There is some doubt—but not much—that the increase in world demand for energy will have its own steady effects in the market. Slowly the coming of higher prices as fuel resources begin to shrink and the need to offset many externalities is met will promote frugality. Slowly the wasteful consumption of energy will dwindle. That has already become clear in commercial and industrial use even in the United States, though not yet in residential use.

American consumers will be found to *increase* their savings (possibly only in the form of reduced expenditures as growth declines) as both the key cheap hydrocarbons and public goods such as land, water, and roads rise in price. Falling real incomes will begin to modify private wants, making second cars and gas guzzlers greater luxuries. Well-paid but crowded

Japanese workers, in contrast, will seek more floor space, more public social security, and more green lands as they *reduce* their high rate of savings. These two countries seems likely to approach each other toward some long-term mean.

Excess fuel use in the rich world above 5 kilowatts per head represents a reserve of several terawatts, though one difficult to deploy and hardly decisive in the long run. The Pacific Rim lands have shown the force of continued socioeconomic change on old habits, though not yet in the new direction just suggested, for it is fast growth that has been its driving force, though taking off from the frugality traditional to those countries. Many behavioral changes in energy use and private investment, and in cooking, heating, and especially fast personal transport, will appear even earlier. The subsistence farm families worldwide, our villagers, will turn more and more to local factories and offices for jobs with more efficient energy consumption, though still at low wages and living standard below the energy knee that we encountered in the previous chapter.

Energy at the End of the Rainbow

Should conventional fuel supplies lag greatly in the next few decades—a not very likely case—it is not imprudent to foresee the swift growth of one or more new energy sources, all promising large-scale use fifty years hence if development is pressed. None are obvious winners in the next few decades; still, it is shortsighted to ignore all possibility for a novel source of real importance. We sketch here the possibilities for a few energy rainbows.

Four or more decades from its still-uncertain technical realization, fusion energy does promise a more or less unending fuel resource if it ever comes, and an extraordinarily large resource—some 1,000 terawatts a year for each square kilometer of deep ocean (from which the needed deuterium can be extracted)! The need for auxiliary lithium perhaps sets an earlier limit on the initial exploitation of a deuterium-based thermonuclear cycle, but if it does, the fusion reactions can be modified at some cost. It is the management of radioactive wastes, even though they are less by a factor of twenty than those from fission, and the very high capital costs that can most limit fusion. The first international prototype of a large commercial fusion power plant is tentatively planned now for 2015 at the earliest.

But we see other possibilities:

• High gains in efficiency could result from burning coal at high temperatures, thus extending the largest of all fossil fuel resources. Probably such an effort would be based on fluidized-bed technology, perhaps on generating or using heat even within the underground coal seam itself or as coal gases to be shipped out for fuel.

• Much wider use of fossil methane might ensue from very deep-lying natural gas fields, perhaps even primordial and abundant ones, or from known large but inaccessible ocean-floor methane deposits. Gas turbines are efficient for both fixed and mobile use, and the greenhouse gas released per unit energy from burned methane is much lower than that from coal, and only about half that of oil. The total methane resource, not at all well known, is probably greater than all oil resources, possibly far greater.

• Methane is itself a potent greenhouse gas, and control of its loss during distribution is sure to become mandatory and to raise its costs. Hydrogenous fuels like natural gas, gas from coal, and methyl and ethyl alcohols— pure hydrogen is the extreme case, of course—allow more efficient use. Fuel cells, now workable though quite high in capital cost (they have long powered the space shuttle orbiter), produce electric power directly from such gases and oxygen. Their main waste is innocuous water vapor, with some carbon dioxide. Most hydrogenous fuels, however, are *not* primary energy sources but must be made by sunlight or the use of other sources of power. They can be shipped and stored on a large scale once the supply is economical. Stored energy at small scale, now provided laboriously to villagers in the form of wood lots, crop waste, and kerosene, is one place where novel technology—photovoltaics that generate hydrogen from water fed to fuel cells—would open wide a new solar-based supply anywhere under the sun.

• Fission energy from uranium, using future breeder reactors to extend the earth's uranium resource tenfold or more, might surpass even coal in total energy yield. Fission makes no carbon dioxide; it could be used for creating steam or making hydrogen. Calamitous accidents remain possible, and radioactive fission waste demands safe disposal; wide public acceptance will depend on reassuring experience with new types of safer reactors, and on widespread urgency of need.

• Local supply of power from sites favorable to windmills, waves and tides, and geothermal heat will surely increase, but these are geographically determined and can hardly supplant fossil sources.

Large-area photovoltaic conversion into electricity of desert sunlight (not for the vicinity but for distribution to distant populations) and its solar parallel, power generated afloat far from land using the natural ocean temperature gradients in the hot equatorial seas, are both attractive schemes on paper. Neither is fully developed although some trial installations exist. Both power sources can deliver synthesized fuel or fertilizer (hydrogen, methanol, ammonia, urea) to be used ashore after bulk transport over oceanic distances. Air and seawater provide all the raw materials. Direct delivery of electric power for immediate use on land as it is generated is a possible option, but seaborne sources cannot supply continual power by cable very far from shore.

Compromises

So far the word *sustainability* has hardly entered our pages. We cannot dissemble our pragmatic view that first things come first; as John Maynard Keynes famously said, in the long run we are all dead. But we do look as far as a century and more ahead, and while we do not claim to foresee the third millennium, we do not wish to promote a merely transient fix. Sooner or later the future will arrive with its due bill.

We took note in chapter 1 of generational differences in priorities, such that the present authors are old enough to see as the first priority the artful construction of a regime of common security, a world of nations so linked as to minimize the dangers of war, above all of nuclear war at large scale. The generation that came to awareness after World War II weighs more heavily the long run of population growth. That is a crisis demonstrably behind us, ever since the percentage rate of increase worldwide peaked a little before 1970. The cheap and expert control over death by pestilence, especially for infants, simply preceded the control over births. We now bear the burden of a rapid social transition; the world population is double that of World War II years, and another near doubling is clearly on the way.

Yet the next concerned generation views as a major threat the protracted lack of equitable development: one-fifth of humankind remarkably and visibly well off, four-fifths almost as poor as ever. The billions must and will live better, and they demand growth, up to all too visible limits. We have put forward a scheme for Common Development among nations that can use the savings from warfare to initiate the move toward equity, until at last global equality will be within reach, if perhaps only toward 2100, after a stable or slowly falling world head count.

This last generation has also grasped the deepest threat to human welfare, the welfare of the surface of our planet and its resources, especially the atmosphere and waters we share, and the living intricacy of the biosphere of which we active humans are so powerful a part. The youngest see the damaging impact of our aggregate human activities: for the first time the human economy is finding global limits, now that we are so many and so active that the effects of our deeds have risen to global scale. Sustainability recognizes that no population can be allowed unlimited growth of action on the finite surface of a close-coupled world. The time scale of such limits is not at all well defined, but it becomes essential to judge them aright.

We offer a compromise among the priorities of these three generations, all persuasive.

• Without peace the nations are too easily able to destroy everyone's hopes and even the global environment. The oil wells of Kuwait, set on fire by the retreating Iraqis, light that truth, although their scale was mostly local. A secure peace and its lasting implementation come first. That is both the most urgent task and the smallest. We intend to begin the world to come by building a Common Security regime within the next twenty or twenty-five years.

• Can peace be maintained solely by treating the dire symptom of war? That peculiarly human plague should be fought nearer to its social and economic origins. Among them what we can best modify is the global inequality of life and of hope. The effort and capital once spent on over-preparation for war, when released, can begin to fund a world of Common Development. The rich cannot neglect the many others who breathe their common air, nor those who might use war to redress or even to avenge their long exclusion. Common Development, sharing the burden of savings and effort toward a fairer world, offers shared goals to all, tangible gain, and high hopes. They will come slower than a practical Common Security system; let us aim for conspicuous, even decisive, gains, though not anything near completion even by midcentury.

• Even if generously funded by aid and investment, the policy of Common Development is not guaranteed to succeed. Even though each attracts roughly equal levels of per capita investment from abroad, China is showing much faster progress than Mexico. The prosperity of the smaller East Asian lands, achieved almost without the benefits of foreign aid, is growing much faster than, say, that of heavily supported Tanzania. The Marshall Plan remains the only historically successful example of internationally financed economic development. Plainly money alone is necessary but not sufficient to realize our goal of a fairer and so more peaceful world. Common Development is not utopian even with the present state of the world as initial condition, but only if it garners the focused and persistent support of most nations, North and South alike.

The Environmental Limits

Human well-being in the long run depends on the structures and rhythms of the planet—the state of the air, the sea, the soil, and the life they bear. Many hold that the gaseous products of the fossil fuels we have burned ever since Tudor times are by now enough to warm disastrously the global climate. So far no clear sign of that potential warming has yet been seen above the natural noise in the complex climatic system. We think it most prudent to aim first at alleviating the short-term decisive human issues, war and poverty. However, addressing them successfully seems to us a necessary but not sufficient condition for any approach to long-run sustainability for a species that fills a shifting but finite niche.

Without a working regime for peace, without lively hope for a better life for the billions, those increasing ranks of the poor will not exert the political will to deny themselves what we, the rich, have had in superfluity, our energy-based growth of affluence. First things first; keep hope alive as we move toward a better and fairer regime of frugality and efficiency. Then we can confront under global consensus the environmental problems whose advent and whose remedy must be found on still grander a scale. We have most of a century to find our way, and of course we need to keep a steadily more vigilant watch for earlier signals of environmental trouble.

The planet Venus is a runaway greenhouse, oven-hot under a nearby sun. The largest change we humans have introduced on a planetary scale is a contribution of greenhouse gases to the mix of trace gases in the atmosphere. Water vapor is the main greenhouse gas. Even though a minor constituent of the air provided by nature—water vapor usually accounts for under ten grams of every kilogram of air—that highly variable "impurity" dominates the weather, controlling sunlight, cloud, and wind. The carbon dioxide in the air is about thirtyfold less abundant than is water vapor. But it is both the essential chemical nutrient for all green plants and the second determiner, after water, of the vertical transport of infrared radiation, a major process in the regulation of climate. It is a dominant part of the atmosphere of lifeless Venus.

Humans add carbon dioxide to the air every time we burn long-buried carbonaceous matter for fuel, or convert old standing forests to grass or cropland. The bubbles of antique air deep in the ice cores that scientists collect from the polar caps do show in the last forty years a worldwide increase of about 25 percent over the preindustrial level of carbon dioxide, and a close relationship between that level and the use of carbonaceous fuel year after year.

The climate system, the seas, the adjustment of all life forms to changed conditions, complicated feedbacks among water vapor, clouds, air temperature, and much more, place our present prediction of the consequences of increases in carbon dioxide beyond certainty. We are sure that in itself it tends to heat the surface of the Earth by trapping some radiation, but we do not understand all the intricate side phenomena that follow. Many scientists think a world temperature increase of a few degrees farenheit will follow a doubling of this trace gas. Other gases released by human activity, mainly methane, nitrogen oxides, and certain Freon-like molecules, must also be considered. Even the effects of that warming, if it took place, are beyond sure calculation, but they include a rise in world sea level by a matter of a couple of feet, complex weather changes, and new crop conditions.

Modern weather records, themselves intricately variable, show no clear sign of global warming during the last decade when carbon dioxide levels have been highest. Until nations can see the reality of the effects, and cost out plausible remedies, we doubt that the poor world will forego what we rich have so long nurtured, our affluence largely based on the growth of fossil energy use.

Table 10.1 shows the expected carbon dioxide content of the atmosphere given the world energy use we foresee during the twenty-first century. A gigaton of carbon burned releases that amount of the gas into the air, but it does not remain there long. Retention by the air is from 40 to 50 percent; we have taken that into account. (The rest may go to the ocean, but there is still some uncertainty as to where it actually resides.) This slow estimate of change, a doubling that takes more than a century, is good news. It derives from our prudent estimates of how fast the billions of fast growers and villagers can in practice become energy richer, not from any limits arbitrarily imposed out of concern for world climate. But our esti-

Table 10.1
Estimated carbon dioxide in world air (measured as carbon content)

	Gigatons of carbon content
Preindustrial	600
1950	660
1995	770
2025	890
2065	1,100
2090	1,200

Source: Authors' calculation based on their estimate of world energy use.

mate turns out to allow for reasonable growth. Even our villagers can enjoy the 1.5-kilowatt benchmark of comfort without ominous threat to the global climate.

Naturally a close watch is imperative to decipher a warming signal above the background noise. But the moderate rate of increase in carbon dioxide levels so far, and the very large world economy that will stand in place to alleviate bad outcomes—say the flooding of south Florida, the Netherlands, and coastal Bangladesh that could result from a sea-level rise of a couple of feet—is reassuring. Carbon dioxide may cost our kind lots of effort, but it does not appear to present a sure barrier to all hopes of a workable world. In the longer run, new energy sources and frugality will come more and more into play. This risky time of transition appears more hopeful than we had a right to expect.

The Limits of Reason

Our guides over all these pages have been two: first reason and then empathy. We have no doubt that those two, the chief resources for planners and proposers, in no way exhaust what is open to art, to events, to human history. In that spirit we want to describe at some length a curious and exemplary event of decisive local importance that our merely rational models do not seem able to anticipate. Let it stand as the kind of process that reality will bring in abundance, once these pages are confronted with what actually took place among 10 billion humans in the midst of a century that is yet to begin.

Manuel Antonio the Reborn

Once again we enter the domain of real historical events beyond mere abstract description by counting and logic.[4] These events are archaic in nature but recent all the same: they took place during the last ten years. The drama opened in 1989, in one poor province of one very poor country, Zambézia province in north-central Mozambique, in southeastern Africa inland from the Indian Ocean. The events exemplify both the limitations and the power of a reasoned analysis of war, peace, and polity.

The prophet Manuel Antonio was a small man with "an innocent and gentle face"; he wore fatigues and a military beret, its only badge a wooden cross. He was already a received prophet when a British journalist interviewed him in 1991 at a rally near a provincial capital in central Mozambique. Manuel quietly explained: "I was reborn . . . I am the son of Jesus Christ . . . I don't act like a soldier . . . Besides all this, I heal the sick." His program began with a simple, spectacular rite: the prophet spoke to the crowd in a loud voice from a shallow grave that his supporters dug. He lay down and was loosely covered as all watched. Of course it was no deception but a meaningful reenactment, a symbol as dramatic as the crucifix itself.

For everyone knew Manuel Antonio's story. He had died some twenty years before from some familiar fever, like so many of his fellow citizens. But almost alone among so many had he risen from the grave, enjoined by Jesus to carry a message of hope to the people of Mozambique. That message was a call to courageous resistance, given strength by a wonderful vaccine against bullets called *naparama*, administered by rubbing certain ashes into a few small cuts in chest or neck. His unique message spread very widely once he came; in its wake the young men of much of central Mozambique rose to march again and again as a part-time army, to fight off the terrible plague of bullets. Their uniform was a red ribbon; but they came by tens of thousands to support the government's militia who, once willing to fight, could use their real firearms, weapons explicitly denied to his followers by Manuel Antonio.

Manuel Antonio's vaccine would go far to end the deadly plague of bullets. The indigenous vector of that plague was after all only another irregular infantry of ten or twenty thousand young men. Hundreds of fast-moving, well-armed platoons—sometimes even at battalion strength, up to 1,000 soldiers—of young men were led, supplied, and loosely coordinated by the implacable forces opposing the government called RENAMO (Resistencia Nacional Mocambicano, also MNR). They were mimicked as well by no small number of armed entrepreneurs, "social bandits."

RENAMO, like Manuel Antonio himself, had been summoned to move among the people by a powerful agency quite external to Mozambique. Its forces were first recruited and armed in 1976 by the intelligence service of Northern Rhodesia. In 1980 at the collapse of that transient settler state, RENAMO assets were inherited—and their toughest fighters flown to training camps to the south—by the security services of the Republic of South Africa. Under Pretoria the forces of RENAMO grew more than tenfold over the next years, to some 10,000 active combatants, and as many more in training or reserve. The neighbors of the Republic took a strong interest in destabilizing rural Mozambique. Its wide plains had often provided refuge for the armed partisans of majority rule in the white-run states. Early on the rebels had even threatened Malawi's rail link to the sea, and black-ruled Malawi, to help protect its trade, tolerated RENAMO for a while.

RENAMO troops usually bore modern assault rifles and carried explosive charges along with their machetes and spears. Armed, hungry, teenaged, and ruthless, trained and told to destroy, that is what they did. High power lines, schools, clinics, ambulances, nurses, teachers, foreign relief workers, supplies—any sign of the national government—were priority targets. But they did not hesitate to massacre whole villages, to maim and mutilate most cruelly, or to kill anyone who resisted them, indeed, at times any who caught their eye, from grumbling old women to wide-eyed young children. The foreign community soon came to consensus: RENAMO's civil war raged for a decade as "an unmatched barbarity."

This attack on the villages of the country was remarkably successful. Estimates suggest that RENAMO blew up a third of the power pylons in the country, and destroyed or forced the abandonment of close to half the rural primary medical care network. Three million of the 14 million rural people of Mozambique, who make up 85 percent of the population, fled to refugee camps for foreign-supplied food and the rather timorous protection of the 40,000 or 50,000 government troops of FRELIMO (Frente de Libertacion de Mocambicano). By U.N. estimates in late 1990, some

900,000 people had died, most of them women and children, during the long disorders, certainly much aggravated by two or three years of drought that had withered the untended fields across the wide plateau, twice the area of California. The short life span of the people of Mozambique was in terrifying decline, down by five years or more out of less than forty. The demography was ruled by the disorder.

Manuel Antonio raised young men by the ten thousand from poverty and idleness around the refugee camps. Immunized by his magic against bullets, and inspired to regain their homes, the refugee youth poured out to meet each RENAMO raid in overwhelming numbers, even though Manuel's fighters bore only spears and knives. What had been a cruel sport—quickly dispersing a hundred families of fearful villagers—became a real gamble for RENAMO. Each attack by a well-armed company of a hundred men would have to beat back again and again a horde of newly unafraid, angry, shouting, spear-bearing strong young men, tens of times their number, though without any guns. RENAMO suffered losses; it no longer enjoyed free indulgence in terror. Often enough the rifle-bearing FRELIMO government regulars, once again ready to fight, would arrive in time to complete the defense of some settlement.

Hundreds of villages were resettled under the prophet's lead by their old residents. RENAMO began to lose its unchallenged initiative of countryside terror. Even after the end of 1991, when Manuel Antonio was himself verifiably killed among his acolytes while "defending a coconut plantation" and his body taken to the provincial capital to bear witness to its bullet holes and stab wounds,[5] the dominance of RENAMO continued to dwindle. Of course in the meanwhile, the rains had returned and the sponsoring government in Pretoria had sharply changed course. Overseas instigators had lost interest in the barbarities; arms and money and possibly even advisors had dwindled away. The fortunes of war had shifted for good.

By October 1992 RENAMO and the FRELIMO government met in Rome and signed an agreement for peace. The *naparamas*, those "irresistible forces" of Manuel Antonio, began to disperse. The military gains under the prophet had been solid, never rivaled by the FRELIMO army, not with its confused regulars, first under Eastern European, then North Korean, and finally under British trainers; not by its uncertain, even duplicitous, armed village militia; not by its well-paid if few foreign mercenaries; not even by the Zimbabwean and Zambian regular army units. (Those African neighbors had entered the fray, to be sure, mainly in the limited role of guarding their own rail links to the sea.)

In October 1993, a year of approximate peace was certified on the spot in the capital Maputo by U.N. Secretary-General Boutros Boutros-Ghali. No secretary-general had ever before come to the new country. U.N. plans are firmly on paper, and entail money to spend for demobilization of the contestant forces and the raising of a new army of national unity; resettlement financed en masse for farmers, with a new supply of seeds and hoes to till the newly green lands; and monitored national elections held in 1995. RENAMO has been funded by the United Nations to turn itself into a political party in the new parliament.

The blue helmets are on the scene: 6,000 U.N. soldiers under the French name ONUMOZ patrol the roads and the rails to keep the peace. They come from Bangladesh, Brazil, Botswana, Italy, Japan, Uruguay, and Zambia. The new presence is of the same polyglot style as the trainers, relief workers, advisors, and experts civilian and military who have thronged to warring Mozambique for almost twenty years, from capitals around the world on errands of war and peace alike. Negotiators will set a date for actual demobilization, and a new peace for Mozambique will, or perhaps it will not, begin. As we close our text, the peace holds, FRELIMO is a part of the coalition government after supervised elections, and foreign donors have sent farmers back to their fields with tools and seed; even the rains have continued. Of course the history of this land has not ended.

The arguments of this book are based quite generally on calculations of gain and loss for those simple ends most people cherish: peace, long life, economic well-being, even justice. Many readers will remain skeptical, citing the evident role of pride, hate, greed, revenge, aggression—a whole catalogue of by no means mild responses. It is to attend to these appropriate doubts that we have told this narrative of Manuel Antonio of Zambézia province, his divine instruction on the mountain, and his vaccine against bullets.

It would be foolish, even absurd, to pretend that two MIT physicists might have assessed the civil war in Mozambique well enough to foresee the kind of change brought by Manuel Antonio. The unpredictability of history surely shapes this story, and we would not and cannot deny it. But there are limits as well to the sway of chaos; precedents and causal circumstances are here in part.

First, inspired military prophets are nothing new to history. They have appeared to relieve the miseries of the people in many places and many epochs. Perhaps the Tai Ping rebellion of the 1850s in China, a movement that organized an army of a million against the emperor, remains the largest accomplishment of a self-avowed heaven-sent leader; he too was a professed Christian. Related events in the local Shona traditions of Mozambique have occurred as well, chronicles of a number of past curers who held charms against those alien and inaccessible bullets.

The tactical aptness of a strong social impetus that encouraged many to accept the risk of resistance is exactly what was needed against RENAMO's force. Always much outnumbered, yet always on the attack, the guerillas were bound to draw back from any locus of real resistance. Single individuals resist at high risk, but the odds began to favor any village that included a large number of young men who fought back even at their own peril. The stings of a few dying bees do defend the hive.

Nor was it the battle for village safety alone that counted. The decline of enthusiastic support from far-off Pretoria began in the same years as the new peasant resistance under Manuel Antonio took the field. Even if the South African security forces were not always in close step with political change, even though RENAMO and its emulators certainly did not march only to the orders from distant sponsors, all the changes were in the right direction. Doctrinaire centrally promulgated reforms of the village economy, which had damaged the resilience of traditional social structures, were also fading as transforming events in Africa and in Eastern Europe took effect in the mid-1980s. It was a new reforming non-Marxist president of FRELIMO, Joaquim Chassano, who began talks with RENAMO in the late 1980s. Even the weather helped in the end; once the fields turned green under welcome rains, the refugee farmers longed for home. But although we can point to these influences on the outcome, it would be self-deception to ignore that extraordinary prophet who rose from the grave.

As we close this text in the spring of 1998 we can report that Mozambique, still very poor, is green now and broadly at peace. The situation continues to astonish us with surprises that pass beyond our reasonable extrapolations. One wealthy American was a zealous supporter, private donor, and public advocate for fearsome RENAMO over the years of its long campaign. Now this same man is planning to invest in a new and large national park that encompasses glistening ocean beaches and Maputo River savannah, where prosperous tourists will ride in sumptuous railroad cars amid elephants and lions in restocked lands once decimated by war—someday. History allows the wide unfolding of themes over a few centuries, but it hardly supports direct prediction within one land for even one decade.

Coda

The wisest of historians today appear to hold that the predatory nature of human beings is innate. Of course that predilection marks every age; Hegel was not the first nor the last to see history as slaughter bench, and human memory is long. Yet Manuel Antonio's tale shows that in turn predators attract their own hunters. Reason and concern can tilt the balance still more against cruel trends, since both wealth making and weapons have so much improved. Few of those who have become well-to-do will seek perilous adventures, and the venturers and the vengeful alike will gain less from war than from peace.

Pestilence, too, is a danger not under full control. Viruses of AIDS and the deadly flu are the examples of our century. They will not be the last; but it is no folly to imagine that our control will spread to most new scourges as it has so decisively beaten back other microbial enemies. The future can be more peaceable and healthier, even though neither war nor disease nor the power of unreasonable institutions old and new will vanish. We stand on that reasonable ground, against the historians.

What is left for hopeful projectors (who do not claim to be prophets) to say appeared in print for the first time long ago, the aphorism of a young radical philosopher Karl Marx, not yet thirty-five. His words have been written on the walls all over Mozambique in the last decades by supporters of FRELIMO, although as a rule only the first stirring phrase was painted up. It seems still a wise account of how events proceed, especially apt for how they might be dimly, oh so dimly, foreseen.

The people make their own history, but they do not make it out of new parts, nor under circumstances of their own choosing, but rather out of what is immediately before them, found, given, and handed down.[6]

What we who try to forecast know of the future comes down to this: a few parts, we hope important ones, from that all-conditioning past. What is handed down is potential. It will be at best realized only in part. But an opportunity has opened, we argue, unique in the few hundred centuries of our species.

After this coming century or so of grand transition, we expect that our kind will touch the effective end of most material and population growth and a distinctly new regime will arise, once more growing from its own historical roots. During the decades just before and just after the year 2100, we expect much slowed rates of growth, both for world population and for world economic activity. The long-continued increase at several percent per year will fall not to zero but to a fluctuating value averaging below 1 percent. The much larger economy—we hope both more efficient and more frugal—will be able to absorb without visible overall increase the remaining local growth required by the populations left behind. The overall rates will depend upon the global environment and on the choices of the population.

This merely quantitative outcome would imply profound changes in the economic categories dominant since the twelfth century or so in the North. As occurred once before in medieval times, before the period of modern growth began, the interest owed to capital and the net profits from economic production will both become minimal, no longer of much importance to a society at a plateau of aggregate size, or from time to time slowly decreasing. Tracing that new pattern is a task for others.

We end with the simple remark we have tried to demonstrate: there is reason enough to hope.

Notes

Chapter 1

1. David Holloway, *Stalin and the Bomb: The Soviet Union and Atomic Energy, 1939–1956* (New Haven: Yale University Press, 1994), pp. 109, 176–177.

Chapter 2

1. For an illustration and definition, see Massimo Livi Bacci, *A Concise History of World Population* (Cambridge, MA: Blackwell, 1992), pp. 16–22.

2. See World Resources Institute, *World Resources 1994–1995* (New York: Oxford University Press, 1994), which presents a graph on the percentage of world population percentage growth that peaks in the late 1960s at about 2.1 percent per year and falls to an estimated 1.5 percent in 2000.

3. See Sergei Petrovich Kapitza, *Uspekhi [Physics]* (January 1996), pp. 63–80. His forthcoming book will appear from Springer in 1998 or 1999.

4. Alfred W. Crosby, *Epidemic and Peace, 1918* (Westport, CT: Greenwood Press, 1976), chap. 5.

5. *Statistical Abstracts of the United States* (Washington, DC: U.S. Government Printing Office, 1993), table 1376.

6. Ibid., chapter 11, pp. 207, 215.

7. Vaclav Smil, *China's Environmental Crisis* (Armonk, NY: M.E. Sharpe, 1993), pp. 16–22.

8. A. Coale, "Fertility and Mortality... with Special Attention to China," *Proceedings of the American Philosophical Society*, vol. 132 (1988), p. 185.

9. Quoted in Richard Rhodes, *The Making of the Atomic Bomb* (New York: Simon & Schuster, 1986), p. 778.

10. William M. Arkin, "Nuclear Notebook," *Bulletin of the Atomic Scientists*, January/February 1995, pp. 69–71; March/April 1995, pp. 78–79.

Chapter 3

1. Ashton B. Carter, John Steinbruner, and Charles Zraket, eds., *Managing Nuclear Operations* (Washington, DC: Brookings Institution, 1987).

2. William A. Arkin, "Nuclear Notebook," *Bulletin of the Atomic Scientists,* January/February 1995, pp. 69–71; March/April 1995, pp. 78–79.

3. See the treaty text in *SIPRI Yearbook: World Armaments and Disarmament 1993* (New York: Humanities Press), pp. 549–554.

4. Arkin, "Nuclear Notebook."

5. The Reserve-staffed system was put on an on-call basis between 1992 and 1995, and is still so held.

6. U.S. Department of Defense, *Annual Report of the Secretary of Defense to the President and the Congress, 1996*, appendix D-1 and D-2.

Chapter 4

1. U.S. Department of Defense, *Annual Report of the Secretary of Defense to the President and the Congress, 1996*, appendix J.

Chapter 5

1. Immanuel Kant, *On Perpetual Peace* (New York: Liberal Arts Press, 1973).

Chapter 6

1. Nelson Mandela, *Long Walk to Freedom* (Boston: Little, Brown, 1994), pp. 505–507.

2. Lloyd Dumas, "Organizing the Chaos," *Bulletin of the Atomic Scientists,* November 1993, p. 46.

3. In 1944 the members of the United Nations, meeting at Bretton Woods, a resort hotel near Mount Washington in New Hampshire, founded the International Bank for Reconstruction and Development, informally known as the World Bank, and the International Monetary fund as independent agencies to facilitate recovery after World War II.

4. The U.S. Congress passed the Byrd Amendment in 1971 permitting imports of strategic Rhodesian raw materials such as ferrochrome, used for special alloy steels.

5. Iraq's invasion of Kuwait triggered, two days later, U.N. Security Resolution 661, which codified trade and financial sanctions.

6. In the summer of 1950 North Korea invaded South Korea militarily. In response the United Nations, largely at U.S. request, organized a multinational force to defend South Korea.

7. *Daedalus*, American Academy of Arts and Sciences, summer 1993.

8. *The Military Balance 1995–1996* (London: Institute for Strategic Studies), p. 269.

Chapter 7

1. Robert L. O'Connell, Sacred Vessels: The Cult of the Battleship and the Rise of the U.S. Navy (Boulder: Westview Press, 1991), p. 315.

2. Report by Thomas Friedman in the *New York Times*, 1995.

3. *The Military Balance 1995–96* (London: Institute for Strategic Studies), p. 48.

4. U.S. Department of Defense, *Annual Report of the Secretary of Defense to the President and Congress*, 1996, pp. 18, 150, table IV-2.

5. Note that the *Annual Report of the Secretary of Defense 1996* schedules only eleven active carriers by 2001; see table IV-5.

6. The *Annual Report of the Secretary of Defense 1996* projects only fifty such submarines by 2003.

7. U.S. strategic forces consist of nuclear ballistic missiles in silos and submarines and long-range bombers carrying nuclear weapons. Included in the cost of their operations and maintenance are communications, early-warning radars, bases, refueling tankers, and testing of nuclear weapons and of the ballistic missiles that carry them.

8. *New York Times*.

9. John M. Lee, Robert von Pagenhardt, and Timothy W. Stanley, *To Unite Our Strength: Enhancing the United Nations Peace and Security System* (Washington, DC: University Press of America, 1992).

10. *SIPRI Yearbook 1995* (New York: Humanities Press), p. 389 ff.

Chapter 8

1. World Resources Institute, *World Resources 1994–1995*, table 21.2.

2. Global exports range from $60.7 billion in 1950 to $5 trillion in 1995, while imports went from $63.6 billion in 1950 to $5.1 trillion in 1995 (*U.N. Handbook of International Trade*, 1995, p. 2).

Chapter 9

1. Vaclav Smil, *General Energetics* (New York: Wiley, 1991), p. 223 ff.

2. World Resources Institute, *World Resources, 1994–1995* (New York: Oxford University Press, 1994), table 18.1.

3. Ibid., table 18.4.

4. Ibid., tables 22.4, 22.5.

5. Ibid., table 18.5 and first few pages of chapter 6.

6. Smil, *General Energetics*, p. 223 ff.

7. *Statistical Abstracts of the United States, 1993* (Washington, DC: U.S. Government Printing Office), table 963.

8. See Vaclav Smil, *Global Ecology: Environmental Change and Social Flexibility* (New York: Routledge, 1993).

9. Smil, in *Global Ecology*, shows that the relationship between power used and quality of life is less than compelling over a wide range. See also Smil, *General Energetics*.

10. Ibid., p. 129.

11. World Resources Institute, *World Resources, 1994–1995*, table 21.2.

12. This forecast is more reliable than many, for the parents are here now.

13. Congressional Budget Office, *Security Through Foreign Aid* (Washington, DC: 1994).

Chapter 10

1. World Resources Institute, *World Resources, 1994–1995* (New York: Oxford University Press, 1994), table 16. 1.

2. Ibid., p. 288.

3. *Statistical Abstracts of the United States, 1993* (Washington, DC: U.S. Government Printing Office), tables 1019 and 1372.

4. William Finnegan, *A Complicated War: The Harrowing of Mozambique* (Berkeley, CA: University of California Press, 1992).

5. Jeremy Harding, *The Fate of Africa: Trial by Fire* (New York: Simon & Schuster, 1993). Harding knew Manuel Antonio personally.

6. Karl Marx, *Der achtzehnte Brumaire des Louis Bonaparte* (Berlin: Dietz Nachfolger, 1885), p. 1; authors' translation.

Index